Access for Windows™ Hot Tips

Roger Jennings

Access for Windows Hot Tips

Copyright© 1993 by Que® Corporation.

Library of Congress Catalog No.: 93-83859

ISBN: 1-56529-234-0

95 94 93   4 3 2 1

Interpretation of the printing code: the rightmost double-digit number is the year of the book's printing; the rightmost single-digit number, the number of the book's printing. For example, a printing code of 93-1 shows that the first printing of the book occurred in 1993.

This book is based on Microsoft Access for Windows Version 1.x.

Acknowledgments

Don Funk of Access Product Support Services (PSS) developed the PSS-KB.HLP file that puts current articles from the Microsoft Knowledge Base into an easy-to-use Windows help file format. Microsoft's Dan Madoni, who developed the Database Analyzer library included in Access, also created the Domain Aggregate Function and Menu wizards described in Chapter 12. Andrew R. Miller, another Access PSS member, wrote the FirstLib library, the subject of several tips in Chapter 12. Helen Feddema, an independent Access consultant, designed the custom toolbar described in Chapter 12. The code examples in Chapter 10 use a naming convention for Access Basic proposed by Stan Leszynski and Greg Reddick of Kwery Corp. Thanks to each of you for making Access easier and more fun to use.

Many tips in this book are derived from questions posed by Access users in the MSACCESS Forum on CompuServe. The contributions of all participants to the MSACCESS forum are acknowledged with gratitude.

Trademarks

All terms mentioned in this book that are known to be trademarks or service marks have been appropriately capitalized. Que cannot attest to the accuracy of this information. Use of a term in this book should not be regarded as affecting the validity of any trademark or service mark.

Microsoft is a registered trademark of Microsoft Corporation.

Credits

Publisher
David P. Ewing

Associate Publisher
Rick Ranucci

Operations Manager
Sheila Cunningham

Publishing Plan Manager
Thomas H. Bennett

Marketing Manager
Ray Robinson

Title Manager
Walter R. Bruce III

Acquisitions Editor
Sarah Browning

Product Development Specialist
Steven M. Schafer

Production Editor
Susan M. Dunn

Editors
Lorna Gentry
Lori A. Lyons
Joy M. Preacher
Midge Stocker

Technical Editor
Michael Gilbert

Book Designer
Amy Peppler-Adams

Production Team
Jeff Baker
Danielle Bird
Jodie Cantwell
Carla Hall-Batton
Heather Kaufman
Linda Koopman
Jay Lesandrini
Caroline Roop
Linda Seifert

Indexer
Joy Dean Lee

Composed in *Utopia* and *MCPdigital* by Que Corporation.

About the Author

Roger Jennings is a consultant specializing in Windows database, word processing, and multimedia applications. He was a member of the Microsoft beta-test team for Access, Word for Windows 2.0, Windows 3.1, Windows for Workgroups, Video for Windows, Visual Basic for DOS, Visual Basic 2.0 and the professional extensions for Visual Basic 1.0 and 2.0, and Multimedia Player 2.0. He is the author of *Using Access for Windows*, Special Edition, and *Discover Windows 3.1 Multimedia*; a contributing author to *Killer Windows Utilities*; and a technical editor for *Using Word for Windows 2*, Special Edition, and *Using Windows 3.1*, Special Edition, all published by Que Corporation.

Roger frequently contributes to Access-related periodicals, including *Access Advisor* magazine and the *Smart Access* newsletter. He also developed a seven-day Access training course for NetBase Computing, Inc. You can contact Roger through CompuServe (ID 70233,2161) or the Internet (70233.2161Wcompuserve.com).

Contents at a Glance

Table of Contents

10 Writing Access Basic Code that Works 149

Introduction

Whether you consider yourself a beginning or experienced Access user, the shortcuts and powerful techniques presented in *Access for Windows Hot Tips* will help improve your proficiency. Here you will find information about the subtle program features you were too busy to read about in the documentation. You also will find undocumented secrets, tips, and proven advice.

Unlike some computer books, reading the chapters or tips in this book in any particular order isn't necessary. Each chapter includes tips for a particular feature or function of Access—that is, all tips concerning tables are located in the "Designing and Using Access Tables" chapter, and all macro-oriented tips are conveniently located in the "Using Macros Effectively" chapter.

 Watch in particular for tips identified by a "Hot" icon. These tips are the author's favorites and are bound to pique your interest. You can find a list of the favorites on the inside front and back covers of this book.

Book Conventions

Certain conventions are used in *Access for Windows Hot Tips* to help you understand the techniques and features described in the text. This section provides examples of these conventions. The following table shows special formatting used in this book.

Format	Meaning
italic	Emphasized text and variables
boldface	Text that you are supposed to type
`monospace`	Direct quotations of words that appear on-screen; Access Basic code
`boldface monospace`	Access Basic keywords and type-declaration symbols
`italic monospace`	Replaceable Access Basic variable names
`italic boldface monospace`	Replaceable Access Basic keywords

Keystroke combinations such as Alt+F4 indicate that you press and hold down the Alt key while you press the F4 key. Other keystroke combinations are performed in the same manner.

To use the keyboard rather than the mouse to choose menu options, press Alt and then the letter that appears in boldface in the menu option name. For example, to choose **E**dit **C**ut, press Alt and then E (to access the Edit menu) and C (to choose the option).

CHAPTER

Optimizing Installation and Performance of Access

In this chapter, you find tips that show how to install Access so that you get the features you need without consuming all or a major portion of your available hard disk space. Even if you already have installed Access, you may find the following tips helpful. They explain what files are necessary to run Access efficiently and how to change your AUTOEXEC.BAT and MSACCESS.INI files to improve the speed of Access.

Because Access is a large, memory-hungry application, a group of tips near the end of this chapter is devoted to improving the performance of Access, especially on computers with 4M of RAM.

Use Custom installation when your PC is short on disk space

When disk space is at a premium on your computer, choose the Custom installation option. Access displays the Setup Options dialog, from which you make your installation choices.

Note: The Minimum installation option isn't recommended because it doesn't install the Access help file, an indispensable file even for experienced Access developers.

The following files are recommended to install with the Custom installation:

- Install Microsoft Access and Help. You need the help file because many subjects in the Microsoft Access documentation require searching for help file topics to obtain full coverage of the subject matter.

- Don't install the Cue Cards. Cue Cards are helpful to guide you through your initial use of Access, but the documentation provided with Access is an adequate substitute. For a more detailed tutorial and reference, read *Using Access for Windows*, Special Edition, published by Que Corporation.

  Note: If you want to use the Cue Cards, you also must load the Access help file. If you unmark the Help check box but leave the Cue Cards check box selected, Access loads the help and Cue Card files.

- If you plan to import or attach dBASE, FoxBase, Paradox, or Btrieve files to your Access databases, click the Select button to display the ISAM (Indexed Sequential Access Method) Options dialog. The three ISAM drivers are selected by default. Click the check box for those database file types you don't want to install so that the check boxes are unmarked.

- Install Microsoft Graph and the Sample files. You can delete two sample database files, PIM.MDB and ORDENTRY.MDB, after installation to gain about 850K of free disk space. You need the NWIND.MDB sample database file to follow the examples in the Microsoft documentation.

Delete files you don't need after performing a Complete installation

If you find that you need more disk space but don't need all the functions provided by Access's Complete installation, you can delete the following files safely with File Manager:

- CUECARD.EXE, CUECARDS.DLL, and CUECARD.LES, the files that constitute the Cue Cards feature of Access. After you become familiar with how Access works, deleting these files frees about 1.7M of disk space.

- PIM.MDB and ORDENTRY.MDB, additional demonstration database files not covered by Access documentation. This step frees about 850K of disk space.

- BTRVISAM.DLL (if supplied), if you don't intend to use Novell Btrieve or Xtrieve files. Deleting this file frees 122K.

- PDXISAM.DLL and PARADOX.NET, if you don't plan to use Paradox files. Deleting this file frees 193K.

- DBSISAM.DLL, if you don't intend to import, attach, or export xBase files (dBASE III, dBASE IV, or FoxPro DBF files). You can only import, not attach, FoxPro DBF files with Access Version 1.0. Deleting this file frees 237K.

- STFSETUP.EXE, if you don't need to use the work-group selection feature provided by running STFSETUP with the /w parameter. (Frees 477K of disk space.) Other methods of selecting a workgroup exist than using STFSETUP (see the tip "Use the SystemDB= line to determine your Access work-group" in Chapter 11). Copy STFSETUP.EXE to a diskette before you delete it so that you can reinstall it later.

If you find later that you need these files, you can rerun Setup from your distribution diskettes to reinstall any files.

Note: Most files included on the Access distribution dis-kettes are compressed. Some files must be decompressed and appended to one another to create the final version of the file. Don't try to copy files from the distribution dis-kette to your \ACCESS directory without running Setup.

Reboot manually after installing SHARE.EXE

If you install Access and have Setup add SHARE.EXE to your AUTOEXEC.BAT file, don't choose the Reboot option at the end of the installation procedure. Otherwise, Setup may leave a temporary directory, MS-SETUP.T, on your hard disk.

If you haven't installed Access yet, choose No when asked whether you want Setup to reboot your computer. Reboot your computer manually with Alt+Ctrl+Delete instead.

If you already have installed Access, use File Manager to see whether the MS-SETUP.T directory exists. If it does, delete the directory and the approximately 600K of files it contains; Access doesn't use these files.

Use Stacker or other compression applications with Access

You can use Access with file compression applications, such as DOS 6's DoubleSpace or Stac Electronics' Stacker, that are designed to increase your effective hard disk space. Access is fully compatible with DoubleSpace and Stacker Versions 2.x and 3.x.

The average file compression ratio of your \ACCESS directory after installing Access is about 1.5 for Stacker 2.x and about 1.6 for Stacker 3.x. Stacker compresses Access database files somewhat more efficiently than it compresses executable and DLL files; expect a compression ratio of 2.0 to 2.5 for .MDB files.

Don't run SCHECK if Stacker causes an error #04

When you run early versions of Stacker 3.0's SDEFRAG (disk optimization) application after you install Access, an error #04 message may occur. Stacker then requests that you run the SCHECK application to find and correct the error. According to Stac Electronics' Technical Note #041, you don't need to run—and shouldn't run—SCHECK when error #04 occurs.

If after an error #04 message you run Stacker 3.0 SCHECK application with the undocumented /=D engineering debug switch (such as SCHECK /=D /F), SCHECK reports all lost sector groups and offers to delete them. The lost sector groups reported may not be lost sectors at all but may be valid sectors of your Access database files. Make sure that you respond *NO* when asked whether you want to delete the lost sector groups. If you answer YES, you may damage your database files irreparably.

Set FILES=60 in your CONFIG.SYS file if you use DOS applications

If the FILES= line in your CONFIG.SYS file is set to less than 50, you plan to attach multiple tables, *and* you use various DOS applications under Windows, reserve space for up to 60 file names by changing this line to FILES=60. You will receive a suggestion during Access's installation to set FILES= to at least 50 if FILES=49 or less.

Remove SHARE.EXE if you use Windows for Workgroups

Windows for Workgroups includes a Windows equivalent of SHARE.EXE (the VSHARE.386 driver) that avoids many problems associated with using the DOS version, such as Sharing Violation messages. Windows for Workgroups' VSHARE.386 allocates locks as needed, and doesn't require that you specify the number of locks. The line device=vshare.386 in the [386Enh] section of your SYSTEM.INI file loads VSHARE.386. Thus, VSHARE.386 is active only if you run Windows for Workgroups in Enhanced mode.

If you plan to run Windows in Enhanced mode (the default mode) *and* don't need to retain SHARE.EXE for DOS applications that require SHARE be loaded (such as Paradox), use Notepad or SysEdit to delete or disable the SHARE.EXE line in your AUTOEXEC.BAT file. When Windows for Workgroups loads, it tests to determine whether SHARE.EXE already resides in your computer's memory.

If you don't remove the SHARE line from AUTOEXEC.BAT, you cannot gain the benefit of using VSHARE.386.

Adapt Windows for Workgroups
for use with Access

If you have a version of the network driver for Windows for Workgroups, WFWNET.DRV, dated earlier than 11-02-92, you need to replace the driver with the version of WFWNET.DRV included on the Windows for Workgroups driver diskette that accompanies the Access distribution diskettes. If you use the old driver and use the Network button in Access dialogs to connect to servers that require passwords, you may truncate (lose the end of) the Access database files to which you connect. Choosing **File Repair Database** in Access cannot correct this file corruption.

WFWNET.DRV is located in your \WINDOWS\SYSTEM directory. Use File Manager to check the date of this file. If the date of WFWNET.DRV is earlier than 11-02-92, follow the instructions on the Windows for Workgroups driver diskette to replace the file.

Patch Microsoft LAN Manager
for Access

If you are using Microsoft LAN Manager Versions 2.1 or 2.1a, you need to install a new version of NETWKSTA.EXE in your \LANMAN.DOS\NETPROG directory. The new version fixes a problem that leads to database file corruption that you cannot correct by choosing **File Repair Database**.

The Access distribution diskette for the ODBC Setup in the \LANMAN21 directory includes three different files. The file you copy as NETWKSTA.EXE from \LANMAN21 to your \LANMAN.DOS\NETPROG directory depends on the version of DOS you are using on your workstation. See "Using Microsoft Access with Microsoft LAN Manager" in the README.TXT file for further details.

If you are using a version of LAN Manager earlier than
2.1, you need to change a line in the [workstation] section
of your LANMAN.INI file. (See the same section of
README.TXT in the preceding reference.) If you are using
LAN Manager Version 2.2, you don't need to install the
new version of NETWKSTA.EXE.

Save disk space: Install the ODBC Administrator only if you need it

You don't need to install the Open Database Connectivity
(ODBC) Administrator application (from the ODBC diskette) unless you plan to use Access with the Microsoft or
Sybase versions of SQL Server. You can save about 200K of
disk space by not installing the ODBC application unless
or until you need it.

The files for the ODBC functions of Access are installed in
the \ODBC directory and in your \WINDOWS\SYSTEM
directory.

Make sure that you have enough memory to run Access efficiently

The documentation that accompanies Microsoft Access
states that you can run Access with as little as 2M of
memory (RAM). You need *at least* 4M to achieve only *ac-
ceptable* performance. If you plan to use graphics in your
Access databases or work with large tables, 8M is strongly
recommended.

Remember also that memory is consumed by resident
(TSR) drivers, and applications that CONFIG.SYS and
AUTOEXEC.BAT load before your computer launches
Windows. Network drivers, CD-ROM device drivers
(MSCDEX.EXE), drivers for audio adapter cards and
other multimedia hardware, and substitutes for Program
Manager (such as Norton Desktop for Windows) also can
consume substantial amounts of valuable memory.

If you are running Access with 4M of memory, try the following suggestions to improve Access's performance:

- Don't assign any memory to a RAM disk. A RAM disk is created by an entry in your CONFIG.SYS file similar to

  ```
  device=c:\windows\ramdrive.sys 256 /e
  ```

  Use Windows Notepad or SysEdit to delete or disable this line. Remove any lines in AUTOEXEC.BAT that copy files to the RAM drive.

- Don't use bit-mapped wallpapers for your Windows desktop. Depending on complexity and color depth (256 or more colors), special wallpapers can eat up to 256K of memory. Launch Control Panel (from the Main program group) and then double-click the Desktop icon to display the Desktop dialog. Choose None for the Pattern and Wallpaper combo boxes.

- Set the size of the buffer that Access uses to less than the default value of 512K. Use Windows Notepad to add the line **MaxBufferSize=256** as the last entry in the [ISAM] section of your MSACCESS.INI file, as follows:

  ```
  [ISAM]
  PageTimeout=300
  MaxBufferSize=256
  ```

  See Access's README.TXT file for further details on the use of the MaxBufferSize entry. Chapter 2 describes each section of MSACCESS.INI.

- Open databases for exclusive use, if you aren't sharing the database with others. Access opens databases for exclusive use by default, but you or someone else may have set Access's Multiuser Options to open files in shared mode. Opening files in shared mode consumes additional memory.

- Run Windows in Standard mode. (Change the line in your AUTOEXEC.BAT file that reads WIN to WIN /S and reboot with Alt+Ctrl+Delete.) Remember that you need to use the DOS version of SHARE.EXE if you are using Windows for Workgroups as a client in Standard mode. (See the earlier tip "Remove SHARE.EXE if you use Windows for Workgroups.")

- Allocate a maximum of 512K for SMARTDrive 4.0 or other disk caches. When you installed Windows, the line c:\windows\smartdrv probably was added to your AUTOEXEC.BAT file. With 4M of RAM, the default initial cache size (InitCacheSize) is 1M and the minimum size (WinCacheSize) is 512M. Use Notepad or SysEdit and change the line containing smartdrv to **c:\windows\smartdrv 512 256**. You should find, however, that reducing the cache size reduces the speed of many operations of your other Windows applications. Thus, reserve changes to SMARTDrive 4.0 as the last resort.

Close other applications when you run Access with 4M of RAM

Close other applications if your computer has 4M of RAM and you want to run Access. Otherwise, if you launch Access with another mega app running or launch another mega app with Access running, be prepared for a long wait while Windows reads and writes applications resources stored in your permanent or temporary swap file(s).

Note: *Mega apps* are defined as major Windows applications that have executable (.EXE) files of 1M or larger size.

Use a large, permanent Windows swap file to speed up Access

Some Windows users who have limited free disk space use a temporary swap file rather than a permanent swap file. In Windows Enhanced mode, the swap file (called WIN386.SWP if it's temporary) is referred to as *virtual memory*.

Permanent swap files run more quickly than temporary swap files because of the way Windows reads and writes to permanent swap files. Windows tried to create a permanent swap file when you installed it. Windows suggests that you create a permanent swap file whose size is half the size of the largest block of contiguous disk clusters Windows can find on the drive containing the SYSTEM.INI file. If the files on your fixed disk were highly fragmented before you installed Windows, you may have too small a permanent swap file or no permanent swap file at all.

A permanent swap file should be about 1.5 times the size of the amount of RAM installed in your computer. Thus, if you have 4M of RAM, a 6M permanent swap file is a good starting point. If you plan to attach very large SQL Server tables or dBASE files, increasing the size of the permanent swap file to at least the size of the largest table you expect to attach will improve performance.

Note: This tip doesn't apply to drives that have been compressed with Stacker and other file compression utilities. You cannot create a permanent swap file on a drive running under Stacker. If you created a decompressed DOS partition for a permanent swap file when you installed Stacker, you cannot increase the size of the permanent swap file beyond the size of the decompressed partition.

Increase Access's buffer size if you have 8M or more of RAM

If your computer has 8M or more of RAM and you are working or plan to work with very large tables (such as tables attached from client-server databases), you can speed table and query operations by increasing the maximum allowable size of Access's memory buffer. The default maximum size is 512K. A larger memory buffer allows more table and query data (dynasets) to be stored in RAM rather than exchange data pages with your swap file.

Start by assigning 25 percent of the memory greater than 4M to the buffer and evaluate the performance improvement. If you have 8M of RAM, for example, allocate 1M to the buffer by adding `MaxBufferSize=1024` to the `[ISAM]` section of your MSACCESS.INI file:

```
[ISAM]
PageTimeout=300
MaxBufferSize=1024
```

If you have 12M of ram, allocate a maximum of 2M with `MaxBufferSize=1536`. Access uses the extra buffer memory only when large tables need it. The maximum buffer size you can allocate is 4M.

2

Getting Started with Access Databases

This chapter provides tips that relate to Access as a whole and Access database files. Following the tips for administering your Access database files can prevent very serious problems, especially with secure Access databases.

The first section describes the multiple document interface (MDI) that Access uses to display database objects and other elements of the user interface that may be new to DOS RDBMS users. One section of tips devoted to Access's MSACCESS.INI file includes a description of the changes you need to make to MSACCESS.INI to attach Access libraries. The chapter closes with tips for setting Access's default options.

Use a trackball rather than a mouse

If you're developing full-scale Access applications, consider substituting a trackball for the mouse. Designing forms and reports requires very precise positioning of control objects, such as labels and text boxes. A large diameter trackball (1.5 to 2 inches) makes positioning and aligning objects easier, because more thumb motion is required to move the mouse a given distance. Use the Control Panel's Mouse function to adjust tracking speed.

Note: When you design applications for data entry, make sure that you also can accomplish all operations by using keystrokes. Moving from the keyboard to the trackball slows data-entry operations greatly.

Compact your Access database files periodically

When you delete records from a table, these records are marked as deleted but not removed from the table. Deleting or making major changes in the design of forms and reports often results in orphaned objects remaining in the database. Using Access's compact feature removes the unneeded objects, recovers the disk space the objects occupy, and speeds most Access operations.

Note: Make sure that you have free disk space equal to the size of your database file before you try to compact the file. Access creates a new copy of the database file during the compaction process, even if you use the same file name to compact to. If you use the same file name, the compacted copy replaces the original version on completion of the process.

Use the security features of Access only when you need them

If you are planning to supply the run-time version of Access provided in the Access Distribution Kit (ADK) to users of your Access applications, don't assign permissions until you test the application with MSARN100.EXE, the Access run-time executable file. Run-time Access doesn't enable users to enter Design mode; thus, users cannot modify database objects.

Back up SYSTEM.MDA when you back up your database files

Make a practice of always backing up SYSTEM.MDA along with your database files. Backing up SYSTEM.MDA is an absolute necessity after you implement any of Access's security features. If your SYSTEM.MDA file becomes corrupted and Access cannot repair it, you will not be able to open a secure database, even if you created it.

If you are responsible for administering Access databases on a network, make sure that you back up SYSTEM.MDA in each workgroup directory on your server.

Note: SYSTEM.MDA contains the names of users, their personal identification numbers (PINs), their passwords, and a variety of other information that relates to workgroup membership and security matters.

Make a backup copy of MSACCESS.INI before you make changes

Before making changes to MSACCESS.INI, use Notepad to save a copy under a different name, such as MSACCESS.OLD. Then, if you make erroneous changes to your MSACESS.INI file, you easily can return to using the "plain vanilla" version that Access's Setup application created for you.

Edit MSACCESS.INI to control how Access opens

If you want to control how Access opens and displays its .MDB database files, edit the [Microsoft Access] section of your MSACCESS.INI file. The default entries in the [Microsoft Access] section are as follows:

```
[Microsoft Access]
Filter=Microsoft Access (*.mdb)¦*.mdb¦All Files (*.*)¦*.*¦
Extension=mdb
OneTablePerFile=No
IndexDialog=No
Maximized=1
Tutorial=1
```

You can change the following options in this section:

■ `Filter=` determines the file extensions that appear in the dialogs you use to import or attach. If you want to display Access libraries (which use the extension .MDA) in addition to Access database files for importation or attachment, use Notepad to change the `Filter=` entry to the following:

```
Filter=Microsoft Access (*.mdb)¦*.mdb¦Access
Libraries (*.mda)¦*.mda¦All Files (*.*)¦*.*¦
```

The entire entry must be contained in a single line. This entry is a useful addition when you begin to develop Access libraries that contain form and report templates.

■ `Extension=` sets the default extension (.MDB) for Access database files that Access uses when you enter a new database name without an extension.

■ `OneTablePerFile=` controls how Access treats database files. Access database and client-server databases, such as Microsoft and Sybase SQL server databases, can—and usually do—contain many tables. dBASE and Paradox database files, and worksheet and text files contain only one table per file.

■ `IndexDialog=` determines whether Access displays a dialog in which you can choose from individual index files for a table or database. Index dialogs are used when you attach dBASE and Btrieve tables, but not Access tables that contain built-in indexes.

- `Maximized=` specifies the window style of Access when you launch it. Change the line to `Maximized=0` if you want Access to open in normal (sizable window) style.

- `Tutorial=` determines whether the opening window that enables you to choose Cue Cards appears. When you select the Don't Display this Startup Screen Again check box in the opening window, this line changes to `Tutorial=0`.

Attach libraries and wizards with the [Libraries] section of MSACCESS.INI

The Setup application copies an additional library, ANALYZER.MDA, to your \ACCESS directory but doesn't add the required entry to attach the Analyzer library to Access. When you install the Complete or Custom versions of Access, Setup creates an entry in the `[Libraries]` section of your MSACCESS.INI file that causes WIZARD.MDA, the Wizard library, to be attached to Access:

```
[Libraries]
wizard.mda=ro
```

Note: The `ro` following the equal sign indicates that the Wizard library is read-only. Your application cannot modify tables or other database objects contained in a read-only library.

Add the line **analyzer.mda=** as the last line of the [Libraries] section to attach the Analyzer library. If you don't add a suffix to the equal sign, the library is considered to have read-write attributes. Attaching other third-party libraries and wizards follows a similar procedure.

Add choices to the Help menu to run library functions

By adding a [Menu Add-Ins] section to the MSACCESS.INI file, you can run Access libraries from the Help menu. Making choices from the Help menu is usually more convenient than Microsoft's recommendation to add a command button to a form or report to run the Analyzer library.

So that you can choose Analyzer from the Help menu, add the following section header and line after the last entry in the [Libraries] section in MSACCESS.INI:

```
[Menu Add-Ins]
Anal&yzer==StartAnalyzer()
```

Note: The two equal signs aren't a typographical error; you need the == for the menu add-in to work.

Most other libraries and many third-party wizards also require that you add a line to the [Menu Add-Ins] section of MSACCESS.INI. The documentation or a README.TXT file that accompanies the library gives you the syntax for the entry.

Note: Microsoft recommends the Help menu as the location for menu add-ins because the Help menu does not change when you select a new database object or change from Design to Run mode.

Open databases automatically with a command-line entry

If you are working primarily with a single database file, you can save a step by adding the database file name to the command line so that Access opens the file when you load Access. To launch Access and open the Northwind Traders sample database, for example, follow these steps:

1. Open the Access application group in Program Manager, if necessary, and select the Access icon.

2. Choose **P**roperties from Program Manager's **F**ile menu. The Program Item Properties dialog appears, with **c:\access\msaccess.exe** in the Command Line text box.

3. After the command-line entry, type a space and **nwind.mdb**. The command-line entry now should read `c:\access\msaccess.exe nwind.mdb`.

   Note: If the database file is not in the same directory as MSACCESS.EXE, add the full path to the entry for the database file name.

4. Choose OK to save the entry and close the Program Item Properties dialog.

5. Double-click the Access icon to launch Access. Access opens NWIND.MDB for you.

You can save the time needed to close the tutorial window by clicking its Don't Display This Start-up Screen Again check box. If you want the tutorial window to appear again, change the line `Tutorial=0` to `Tutorial=1` in the `[Microsoft Access]` section of MSACCESS.INI.

Note: Access provides the /Ro and /Excl command-line parameters to open database files as read-only and for exclusive use, respectively. Add one or both of these parameters after the database file name parameter if you want to specify read-only or exclusive use.

Use command-line parameters to enter your user name

For a shortcut logon procedure, use the Program Item Properties dialog to add **/User** *UserName* to the command line that launches Access. *UserName* is the user name you or Access assigned to you (Admin, if you didn't change it).

Note: User names aren't case-sensitive.

Run a macro from the command line when you launch Access

If you want to run a specific macro when Access launches, add /X *MacroName* to the command line in the Program Item Properties dialog. To use this feature, you also must assign a start-up database file in the command line (see the earlier tip "Open databases automatically with a command-line entry" for more details).

Note: If you have written an AutoExec macro, the macro you specify on the command line runs rather than the AutoExec macro.

Keep your password safe; don't use the /Pwd command-line parameter

Access enables you to add your password to the command line with the /Pwd *PassWord* parameter. Making your password visible to anyone who may choose **Properties** from the **File** menu for your Access icon in Program Manger, however, is the ultimate breach of security. *Never* use the /Pwd command-line parameter.

Note: Passwords, unlike user names, *are* case-sensitive.

Review your Access options before you create new applications

Choose View **O**ptions to display Access's default options. Microsoft has done a good job of choosing default values for the nine sets of options you can select from the Category list box. Quickly reviewing the options available in each category pays saved-time dividends when you begin developing major-scale Access database applications.

You may want to change some of these properties, such as the default printer margins, to suit the majority of the applications you write. If you are accustomed to DOS applications that use Enter rather than Tab to move from field to field, for example, choose the Keyboard category. Another Keyboard selection enables you to use the arrow keys to move from character to character rather than field to field when you are entering data.

You need to close and relaunch Access before most of the options you set with View Options become effective. Access sets the default values you choose and reads the MSACCESS.INI file during its start-up procedure. No changes you make to the MSACCESS.INI file take place until you open Access with the newly edited file.

Note: Access stores the changes you make in the View Options dialog in the SYSTEM.MDA file attached to Access. The names of the last four database files you opened also are stored in SYSTEM.MDA. If you use the Setup program to select a different SYSTEM.MDA file, notice that the recent file list (on the Database window's File menu) changes. Any changes you made to the default settings in the View Options dialog no longer apply when you use a different SYSTEM.MDA.

Increase the default font size to make values easier to read

If you run Access in Super VGA (800 by 600 pixel) or Ultra VGA (1024 by 768 pixel) mode, you may have difficulty reading values in Access's default 8-point sans serif font, depending on the size of your display. Choose View Options, select Datasheet from the Category combo box, and try 10-point type.

The default values don't affect Datasheet views of existing tables and queries; only new tables and queries you create show the larger type. Choose Layout Font in table or query Datasheet view to change the size or typeface of existing tables and queries.

Don't set the default Restrict Available Fields option to No in Access 1.0

Update queries cannot work if you set the default value of the Restrict Available Fields option of the Queries category to No. In almost all cases, a general protection fault (another term for an unexpected application error) occurs. If the update query does execute without a GPF, the query likely will update columns incorrectly. Choose View Query Properties to turn off the Restrict Available Fields property of your query, if you need all the fields to be available.

Set the default mode to Shared for opening databases on a network

If you plan to share database files on a network server, make sure that you set the Default Open Mode for Databases property of the Multiuser category to Shared. Otherwise, a single user opening a database in exclusive mode prevents all other users from opening the database. Choose View Options and then select Multiuser from the Category list box to display the Multiuser options.

Note: This tip applies to copies of Access on every workstation with access to shared database files.

Use the No Locks Multiuser option for faster operation

Use the default No Locks value in the Default Record Locking property text box of the Multiuser option for more efficient operation of Access. Especially with large tables, No Locks provides faster operation on networks than

Record Locking. Choose View Options and then select Multiuser from the Category list box to display the Multiuser options.

Note: Don't be misled by the No Locks name. No Locks really means *Optimistic Locking*. The optimistic view assumes that the chances are small that two users of a shared database will try to edit the same record in a table at once. If you try to edit a record that another user is already editing, you see a message box that enables you to choose between overriding the other user's change, abandoning your changes, or saving your changed data to the Clipboard. In the latter case, you can paste the change after the other user releases his or her lock on the record.

Test multiuser locking by running two instances of Access

You can test how Access's three locking choices differ by launching two copies of Access and opening the same database in shared mode. Open the same table in Datasheet view (Run mode). Change the data in the first record in one copy (instance) of Access, but don't complete the change by moving the record selector. Then try making a change in the same record of the other instance of Access. Choose OK when the message box indicates that contention has occurred. Choose a different type of locking; then close and reopen both instances of Access and try the process again.

3

CHAPTER

Designing and Using Access Tables

Traditional databases consist only of collections of tables that contain related data. Access is unique among PC RDBMS because it includes within the database file application-related database objects such as queries, forms, and reports. Conventional DOS and client-server RDBMS use separate applications—usually executable (EXE) files—to display and update data, create and display the results of queries, and print reports. This chapter provides tips for creating and updating Access tables for your database applications.

Designing the table structure of a relational database is a science and an art. The science of the design process is based on a rigorous set of mathematic formulas, called the *rules of normalization*, that define a truly relational database structure. The art of database design involves determining what data to include in which table and deciding how closely to follow the prescribed normalization rules.

One of the principal objectives of table design is simple: Eliminate—or at least minimize—occurrences of duplicate information in relational tables.

Describing the five commonly accepted normal forms of relational tables is beyond the scope of this book. If the term *fifth normal form* sounds like a foreign phrase, invest in a book—such as James J. Townsend's *Introduction to Databases* or George T. Chou's *Using SQL* (both published by Que Corporation)—that explains how to decompose and normalize your data. Que's *Using Access for Windows*, Special Edition, devotes a chapter to database design and the rules of normalization.

Design tables that work efficiently with other database elements

Before you design your tables, make sure that you have at least a preliminary definition of the forms and reports that depend on the tables and queries you create. Creating database applications involves multiple tasks:

- Designing tables to store data with minimum duplication of values

- Designing queries that link tables and select information to be displayed

- Designing forms to display information supplied by the query and update data in tables

- Designing reports to print detail and summary information from the query

Use relation tables to create many-to-many relationships

Access, like other RDBMS, allows only two types of relationships between tables: one to one and one to many. If you have a many-to-many relationship, you need a relation table with a one-to-many relationship to the base tables.

One example of a many-to-many relationship occurs in assigning students to courses. The Students and Courses tables are base tables, which respectively contain one record per student (Student ID is the primary key) and one record per course (Course Number is the primary key). The records in these two base tables contain information about the student and the course, but not what courses the students take. To collect that data, you need a relation table that has one record for each course to which each student is assigned. If each student takes six courses per day, you have six times the number of records in the relation table as in the Students table.

The relation table can have as few as two fields: one for Student ID and one for Course ID. These fields are called *foreign key fields* because they are primary key fields in the base tables to which the relation table is related. Neither field, however, can be a key field in the relation table because you cannot have duplicate values in primary key fields. The relation table creates the many-to-many relationship between the Students table and the Courses table.

You can add fields that contain values unique to two foreign keys in a relation table. A relation table for Students and Courses, for example, can contain a field with the grade that a student received for the course.

Keep field names short to minimize entry errors

You often must refer to fields by name when you create forms, reports, macros, and Access Basic code. Access enables you to use field names up to 64 characters long. Keep your field names short, however, to minimize typing and potential spelling errors.

If you plan to export your tables to xBase files, observe xBase's 10-character field name limit and don't include spaces or punctuation in the name. If you omit spaces, you need not use square brackets to surround the field names in expressions.

Use the default Text field size unless you need more characters

Character fields are Text fields in Access. Access doesn't add trailing spaces to Text fields, and it strips trailing spaces from imported or entered data.

Access Text fields are variable-length; the field size property of a Text field in Access serves only to limit the number of characters you can enter in the field. You therefore can use the Access 50-character default text field size (255 characters is the maximum) without adversely affecting the size of your database file.

Note: If you reduce the size of a Text field by entering a smaller field size value, Access truncates (cuts off) text that extends beyond the new size limit.

Pick a field size that can contain field totals

The SQL aggregate functions that return total (Sum()) and average (Avg()) values for many records require that the field size accommodate the value of the total of the field values for all the records. If you choose the Integer or Single field data types because these fields accommodate the largest value you expect to be entered, users of your application may see a "nocando" message box after adding a hundred or so records and trying to run a total on the field. Refer to the field size table in the Access documentation to determine whether you need a Long integer or a Double-precision size field.

Use Integer or Long Integer field sizes to speed operations

Rather than use the Single or Double field data sizes, use the Integer or Long Integer sizes to speed many database operations. Activities such as arithmetic operations and sorting go faster when you use integers rather than real single- or double-precision numbers. Don't use the Integer or Long Integer field data sizes, however, if your field values include decimal fractions.

Use the Counter field data type judiciously

When you design a table but don't designate a primary key, an Access message box asks whether you want to create one. If you choose Yes, Access adds a field of the Counter field data type to your table, assigns the number 1 to the first record (if any) you entered in the table, and sequentially numbers all subsequent records in the table, including those you add later.

As a result, you cannot set the beginning counter number through any direct method (see the next tip). Further, if you add record 10, for example, and then change your mind and delete it, Access leaves a numbering gap and assigns number 11 to the next record you add.

Note: Question 4 in the PSSKB.TXT file in your \ACCESS directory, "How can I change the starting value of a Counter field?" describes the standard workaround procedure for this action. Look for a more straightforward technique in a future version of Access.

You should find the Counter data type suitable, however, for entering data from sequentially numbered business forms such as invoices and checks, if you prevent deletion of records. (You can prevent record deletion with a macro.) Remember that the Counter field data type is a Long (integer) data type when you refer to it in Access forms, reports, and Access Basic code.

Use Yes/No fields to hold logical data

Logical data can have only two values: true or false. Access substitutes the global constants True and False for xBase's .T. and .F. values. Access equates False with 0 and sets True to the value -1. Although you can substitute an integer field for a Yes/No field, the advantage of a Yes/No field is that you can enter Yes or No, True or False, and even Off or On, in the field; Access translates each of these entries to -1 or 0.

When Access evaluates expressions, the True condition occurs for any nonzero value the expression returns. In the case of expressions, True = Not False. Keep this tip in mind when you use expressions that return numeric values with logical operators, such as Not, Or, and And.

Limit values of data when you specify the Byte data size

If you specify the Byte Field Size property, Access limits entries to the range 0 to 255. Access Basic, however, has no Byte data type. Fields with Byte data size return the Variant subtype 2 (Integer, 2-byte) data.

If you specify the Byte data size, be sure that any values you calculate with Access's built-in functions or create with Access Basic code are limited to the range of 0 to 255. You receive an error message when you try to enter negative numbers and positive values of 256 or greater in a Byte field.

Avoid applying Format properties to Memo fields

Because Memo fields can hold up to 32,000 characters, they often are used to store substantial amounts of text. Don't apply any type of Format property to Memo fields, however, because Access truncates the data in the Memo field to 255 characters. Although the field remains a Memo field, you cannot enter more than 255 characters in the field after applying a Format property.

Use an OLE server application to add or update graphic images in tables

Some Windows RDBMS and most client-server databases have binary large object (BLOB) field data types in which you can store nontraditional data in any form you want. With Access, you need an OLE server application to add or update graphic images. You can use Windows Paintbrush to link or embed bit-mapped images (256 colors maximum). If you need more color depth, use an OLE-compliant image editing application, such as Micrografx Picture Publisher 3.1 or Corel PhotoPaint.

Microsoft didn't include an OLE applet (such as Microsoft Draw) with Access to enable you to add vector-based images to Access tables. If you want to embed or link vector-based images (.WMF, .CGM, .DRW, .DXF, or .WPG files), acquire Microsoft Draw or an OLE server drawing package, such as Micrografx Windows Draw 3 with OLE or CorelDRAW! 3.0. You can use Object Packager, in most cases, if your present drawing or image editing application isn't OLE-compliant. (See the later tip "Use Object Packager to avoid the presentation data size problem" for more information.)

Link rather than embed most graphic and multimedia objects

As a rule, you store graphic images and multimedia objects in the form of files, often on a network server. High-resolution graphic images with high-color (16-bit) or true-color (24-bit) color depths easily can exceed 1M in size. High-quality waveform audio (.WAV) files use more than 10M of disk space per minute in 16-bit stereo format at a 44.1-KHz sampling rate. Embedding these types of data in your Access database can make your .MDB files grow at an alarming rate. Whenever possible, use linking rather than embedding for large objects, no matter what type of data they involve.

Limit the range of worksheet cells used for linking

When you link an Excel worksheet to an OLE object field, Access copies to the Clipboard only the cells you select in Excel's window. You therefore can control the size of the presentation by choosing the range of cells you copy and then paste-link into the OLE object field. When you double-click the presentation (what you see in a form's bound object frame), Access makes the entire worksheet available for viewing and updating. The smaller and simpler the presentation, the faster Access moves between records. You can use just a single cell to create the link to the worksheet.

Use graphs to link Excel worksheets to OLE Object fields

You can create a link to an Excel graph to display the graph in a bound object frame rather than the worksheet on which the graph is based. To create the link, open the

.XLC file, select the entire graph, and copy the graph to the Clipboard. Then paste-link the graph to your OLE Object field. When you want to update the worksheet that underlies the graph, double-click the presentation and then choose File Links in Excel. Select the linked worksheet for viewing or editing.

Use Object Packager to avoid the presentation data size problem

Unless you have a specialized OLE server application, you can avoid the problem of large graphic images by linking the file with Windows Object Packager applet. (Specialized OLE server applications are discussed later in "Use a specialized OLE server for graphics and multimedia objects.") Follow these steps to link a file with Object Packager:

1. Launch File Manager, select the file to link, and then choose File Copy. Click the Copy to Clipboard option button in File Manager's Copy dialog, and then choose OK.

2. Launch Object Packager and choose Edit Paste Link. The application's icon and the linked file name appear in Object Packager's window.

3. In Object Packager, choose Edit Copy Package.

4. Select the field in which you want the linked object; then in Access choose Edit Paste to embed the packaged object that consists of a link to the application and the file.

Note: You cannot paste-link an object created by Object Packager.

Change the link manually if you change the location of a linked OLE Object file

When you create an OLE link to a file in your OLE Object field, the link includes the well-formed path (the drive designator followed by the full path specification) and name of the file. If you change the file's location, the OLE server cannot find the file when you double-click the presentation; you receive a Not Found error message.

The location change doesn't affect the presentation itself, because the presentation resides in the table. You must change the link to the relocated file manually by using the Change Link dialog for the object (choose Edit Object Change Link).

Use a specialized OLE server for graphics and multimedia objects

Lenel Systems (Pittsford, NY) publishes MultiMedia Works, a specialized OLE server used primarily for linking multimedia objects. MultiMedia Works also can link graphic files in a wide variety of standard formats.

With MultiMedia Works, you can create a mini-presentation of a large graphic image (called a *thumbnail*) that enables you to view a scaled version of the image without using all your available disk space. You cannot use MultiMedia Works to edit the graphics file; in most cases, however, you want users to view but not edit the graphic image.

MultiMedia Works enables you to view quickly documents created by popular DOS and Windows word processors. You also can use MultiMedia Works to link analog video clips if you have a video-in-a-window card and a remote-controllable VCR to supply the video signal. MultiMedia Works also supports frame-accurate analog video from computer-controlled laser disc players.

Create a primary key field unless you have a good reason not to do so

If you don't create a primary key field for a table, you cannot establish default relationships with other tables containing related fields, nor can you use the built-in referential integrity maintenance features offered by Access's Relationships dialog. Without a primary key field, even for a single-table database, you receive a `No primary key field` error message every time you change from Table Design to Run mode.

Creating a composite (concatenated) primary key field on a relation table prevents duplicate entries in the relation table. The Student-Course relation table described earlier in the tip "Use relation tables to create many-to-many relationships" provides a good example of how to use a composite primary key field. In this example, you must ensure that you enroll a student only once in a specific course. To prevent duplicate enrollments, you create a primary key consisting of Student ID plus Course ID.

Maintain referential integrity with default relationships

To maintain referential integrity, you must not delete a record on the "one" side of a one-to-many relationship if corresponding records exist on the "many" side. Conversely, you cannot add a new record to the "many" side if no corresponding record exists on the "one" side of the relationship.

If the table on the "one" side of the relationship has a primary key, Access enables you to create default relationships with tables that include a foreign key corresponding to the primary key of a base table. You can tell Access to handle the referential integrity chores by clicking the Maintain Referential Integrity check box when you set the default relationship.

To set default relationships between Access tables, close all database objects and then choose Edit Relationships. Choose the base table from the Primary Table combo box; then open the Related Table combo box and choose the related table. If the foreign key has a different name than the primary key of the base table, you must choose the foreign key name from the Select Matching Fields combo box.

Use a Counter field to display table data in entry order sequence

If you establish a primary key field on any field other than that of the Counter data type, you no longer can display the table data in the order in which it was entered (unless you remove the primary key). To display the data in order entry sequence, add a Counter field to the table and then create a query based on the table. Specify an ascending order on the Counter field in the query.

You need not display the Counter field in the query or a form based on the table. Access updates Counter fields when you append a new record.

Use indexes to speed queries when you have large numbers of records

As you add records to your tables, you may find that running some queries takes longer. Queries that display data in an order other than that of the primary key benefit from an index on the field that you use to specify query sort order. If you don't assign a primary key to related tables, you can add duplicates-allowed indexes on foreign key fields to speed queries. The effect of adding indexes becomes evident when you have a few hundred records in your tables.

Note: When you specify a primary key for a table, Access creates a no-duplicates index on the primary key field. You can verify that this index exists by inspecting the Index property of the primary key field. If you create a composite key field, Access creates a no-duplicates index on the concatenated value of the chosen fields. You need not add a special Index1 concatenated index for the composite primary key.

Minimize the number of indexes to prevent slower data entry

Although adding indexes speeds queries (if the indexes match query sort or selection criteria), indexes slow down table updates such as edit and append operations. Minimize the number of indexes on a single table if data entry speed is a major concern. Each time you change the data in an indexed field or append a new record to an indexed table, Access must update each index when the edits or appends are saved to the table.

Set default values to speed data entry

Access enables you to specify the Default Value property of each field of your table. If, for example, you have an invoice table that contains a date field, you can cause Access to enter the current date in the field when you append a new record. Just add =**Date**( ) in the Default Value text box. Enter =**Date**( ) - 1 for yesterday's date or =**Date**( ) + 1 for tomorrow.

Test for missing entries using Null statements

When you add a new record to a table, Access sets to the Null value those fields that you don't fill in and that don't have default values. The Null value indicates that no data is entered in the field. Conventional PC RDBMS such as dBASE and Paradox, however, don't support the Null value. Instead, they insert 0 in blank numeric fields and spaces in blank character fields. You can test for missing entries (fields that contain the Null value, equivalent to ASCII character 0) with Access's Is Null or Is Not Null operators or the IsNull() function.

Use Validation Rules to maintain domain integrity

The domain of field values is the specified range of values that you can enter in a field. When you add the Validation Rule property to the field, you establish domain integrity for the field. You cannot enter in the field a value that doesn't comply with the validation rule.

One principle of database design is to maintain domain integrity at the table level. The queries and forms that you base on a table inherit the validation rules that you have added to that table. You can override the table Validation Rule property by assigning a new rule for a bound text box or other bound control object on a form.

To conform to established database design practices, don't override table-level validation rules. You must augment Access's table-level validation, however, to ensure domain integrity, as explained in the next tip.

Add a validation macro to ensure domain integrity

You may assume that you can prevent adding records to a table without an entry in a field by adding **Is Not Null** as the Validation Rule property of that field. This assumption isn't true for Access Version 1.0; Access doesn't apply validation rules until you make an entry in the field.

If you tab past the fields with the **Is Not Null** rule and enter a value elsewhere, you can add a new record without entering the required data. This bypass compromises domain integrity. To maintain domain integrity, you need to add a validation macro to test the value of fields with required entries in your data entry form. (Tips on using validation macros are given in Chapter 6, "Using Macros Effectively.")

Use validation text to explain validation rule violations

If you don't enter validation text when you assign a validation rule, when users violate the validation rule they see a message box that reads `The value you entered is prohibited by the validation rule for this field.` Although accurate, this message isn't very informative. Enter the message you want the user to see, such as `You must enter a last name`, as the Validation Text property.

Use the Zoom box to enter complex validation rules

When you enter complex validation rules, such as (**"A" Or "B" Or "C" Or "D"**) **And Is Not Null**, the beginning of your rule scrolls out of view in the property text box. Place the insertion point in the text box of the property you want to enter; then press Shift+F2 to display the Zoom box. Enter your validation rule or text; then choose OK to close the Zoom box.

Change arrow and Enter key behavior to speed data entry in tables

By default, the arrow and Enter keys move the caret (insertion point) from field to field. When you enter many records in table Datasheet view, try changing the Arrow

Key Behavior and Move After Enter options by choosing View Options, and then selecting Keyboard from the Category list box. Change the Arrow Key Behavior property to Next Character to speed editing of typing mistakes. If you leave many blank fields in the records you enter, set the Move After Enter property to New Record. This change enables you to begin entry in a new record without having to move through all the blank fields to do so.

4

CHAPTER

Importing, Attaching, and Exporting Tables

Most Access users have much of the data needed to create Access databases in one or more commonly used PC file formats. Access can import files from other PC database, spreadsheet, and text-editing applications. Access also enables you to export table data in any file format from which you can import a file. You also can attach dBASE III and IV, FoxPro 2.x, Paradox 3.x, Btrieve, and Microsoft or Sybase SQL Server tables. You can view and modify the data in the attached table and retain the file format of the originating application. The tips in this chapter help you avoid some of the common traps and pitfalls of working with imported and attached tables.

Import tables only if you have exclusive file access

If you try to import a shared database file in a multiuser environment and another user has the file open, you receive a message such as `Can't Open FileName` or `Table TableName is exclusively locked.` Access Version 1.0

needs exclusive use of the file during the importing process. After Access successfully imports the file to a table, Access closes the file. Wait until all other users have closed the file, and then import the file's data. In most cases, Access requires only a few minutes to import the data.

Develop applications with imported tables

During the development stage of an application intended to use attached tables, you can import the tables or part of the tables to an Access database for development purposes. When you're ready to test the final application, rename or delete your imported tables and then attach copies (if possible) of corresponding tables. Later, this chapter provides additional tips for attaching tables.

If you plan to attach tables with large numbers of records, you can attach a table temporarily; then design a "make table" action query to create an Access table containing a subset of the records in the table. (See the next chapter for tips on using action queries for this purpose.)

Note: Some Access Basic methods (such as the **Seek** method) apply to tables in Access's native format only. If you use Access Basic to manipulate table records, make sure that the methods you use apply to attached and imported tables.

Add a primary key to tables imported from dBASE files

Unless you have sorted the DBF files you import to Access tables, the records appear in their entry sequence. Add a primary key on the field(s) that you want to use to index the records for display. If you cannot create the desired primary key because of duplicate field values, see the following tip on using a dBASE index to delete duplicate records. Alternatively, you can create a query to sort the table data on any field or combination of fields you want.

Add a counter field to emulate xBase's RECNO( ) function

Access doesn't provide an equivalent of the xBase RECNO( ) function that enables you to identify a record by a sequential record number. Record numbers in Access refer to the relative position of the record as displayed, not the record's entry-sequence number. If you need a cross-reference to the xBase record number, import the file and then add a Counter field to the imported table. Alternatively, add a numeric field to the DBF table and type **REPLACE ALL** *FieldName* **WITH RECNO( )** at the xBase application's dot prompt.

Note: Values of Counter fields in Access tables are permanent. If you delete a record, you create a gap in the record number sequence.

Use SET UNIQUE ON to duplicate key field values in dBASE files

Unlike xBase applications, Access doesn't permit duplicate key field values. If you import a DBF file with duplicate values in the field(s) on which you try to create a primary key, Access displays an error message and refuses to add the primary key. Inspecting candidate key fields of large tables for duplicate values can be quite time-consuming, although you can create a query and sort on the candidate key(s) so that the duplicates are adjacent.

To prevent duplication of candidate key field values in imported DBF files, use SET UNIQUE ON, and then create an index on the key field(s) in your xBase application. Use SET INDEX TO to attach the unique-values index and then copy the indexed file to a new name. By using this process, you lose the records with duplicate key values.

Use Paradox 3.5 format to help convert Paradox 4.0 files

If you need to import a Paradox 4.0 or Paradox for Windows table to an Access database, export a copy of the file from Paradox in Paradox 3.5 format. When you use this process, however, you lose data in fields with newly added Paradox field data types, such as Graphic, BLOB, and Formatted Text.

Avoid import errors by adding values to empty Paradox key fields

If you try to import a Paradox 3.x table with empty key field values, you may see a `Can't have null values in index` message. Use Paradox to add values to the empty fields and then repeat the importation process.

Use Xtrieve data dictionary files to import Btrieve tables

Access needs data dictionary files in Xtrieve format (FILE.DDF, INDEX.DDF, and FIELD.DDF) to open Btrieve table (DAT) files that comprise the Xtrieve database. The Xtrieve FILE.DDF file contains entries that specify the location of the DAT files. If you don't have the required DDF files or if the DAT files no longer are located in the area specified in the FILE.DDF file, you see the message `Couldn't find object 'TableName'`.

Typically, this problem results in Access 1.0 from relocating the DAT files without updating or creating a new set of DDF files that reflect the new location. When this situation occurs, use Btrieve or a third-party Btrieve utility to modify the DDF file or create a new DDF file. For information, see article Q93685, "Couldn't find Object <tablename> with Btrieve files," in the Microsoft Knowledge Base on CompuServe (GO MSKB).

Freeze values when you import worksheets

 Cells that contain formulas in worksheet files appear as blank data cells in the tables you create. Importing a copy of the worksheet that contains values rather than formulas solves this problem. If the range of data you intend to import contains formulas, follow these steps to create a new Excel table with frozen cell values:

1. Select the range of cells you want to import.

2. Choose **Edit Copy** (press Ctrl+C) to copy the selected range of cells to the Clipboard.

3. Open a new worksheet and choose **Edit Paste Special**.

4. Choose the Values option to convert the cells with formulas to values. Choose OK to paste the cell values to your new worksheet.

5. Save the worksheet under a different name.

6. Import the new worksheet file to an Access table.

Avoid errors; ensure that columnar data is consistent before you import

One rule of relational database design is that all data in a field of a table must be of a single data type. Access enforces this rule for imported tables by changing numeric or date values to the Text field data type if it finds a single value in a worksheet that doesn't contain a numeric or date value, respectively. Check to make sure that all the data in each column (excluding row 1, if the first row contains field names) is of the same data type before you import the file.

Avoid using Excel's Database range name when importing with Access 1.0

 Excel worksheets are ideal for importing data to Access tables because of their "database" structure, with field names as the first row of the database range. When you specify a range of cells as an Excel database, Excel assigns the range name Database to these cells. If you specify **Database** as the range name when importing the file, however, Access displays an Invalid Range message box. Select the database range and assign it a new name. Then use the new range name when you import the data.

An easy way to assign a range a name is to open the Define Name dialog by choosing Formula Define Name and selecting Database from the list of names. Type a new name in the Name text box, and click the Add button to create a new named range with the same range as the Database.

Use counter columns as temporary keys when needed

You may need to create several related worksheet files from the source worksheet to import normalized data to Access tables. To recombine the data into one table or a set of related tables, you use key fields to establish the relationships between the tables. You quickly can do so by adding to each worksheet a column with a sequential number. You can use this column—similar to an Access counter field—as a temporary key field for the imported tables.

Use comma- or tab-separated text files for more reliable importing

If possible, use comma or tab characters to separate fields in a text file you plan to import into Access. Text files using comma or tab characters to separate fields import more reliably than fixed-width text files.

You also must establish a text file import specification for Access before you can import a fixed-width text file. All text file import filters use the newline pair (carriage return, CR or ASCII 13, and line feed, LF or ASCII 10) as the record separator.

Inspect the text file in a text editor before importing

If you aren't fully familiar with the characteristics of text files you plan to import, inspect them with a Windows or DOS text editor or text display application. If you see a vertical black bar between fields in a Windows text editor, the bar probably (but not necessarily) represents a tab. If your text application offers it, use hexadecimal mode to verify that the vertical bar is ASCII or ANSI character 9 (a tab), usually 00 09 in hexadecimal display. In the text editor you can see commas used to separate fields in CSV and other comma-separated formats and quotation marks surrounding strings in some mail-merge file formats.

Use the Clipboard to import tabular data more quickly

At some point you may need to import data from various locations in a worksheet to an Access table, or import data in Word for Windows or WordPerfect for Windows tables to an Access table. Using the Clipboard to accomplish this task may be quicker than importing a file. The Clipboard method is especially useful when you don't need to import a large amount of data at one time.

To import data by using the Clipboard, follow these steps:

1. Create an Access table with appropriate field data types and sizes.

2. Copy the selected cells from the source worksheet or document to the Clipboard.

3. Make sure that the insertion point is in the first field of the tentative append record in your new Access table. Then choose **Edit Paste Append** to append the tabular data to your table.

Use the Clipboard to export embedded OLE objects

The Clipboard is the only method in which you can transfer OLE objects embedded in Access tables to other OLE applications. Follow these steps:

1. Click the presentation of the OLE object in Access (whether in table or query Datasheet view, or in Form Run mode).

2. Press Ctrl+C to copy the object to the Clipboard.

3. Launch the OLE compliant application to receive the object.

4. Press Ctrl+V to copy the object to the other application.

Maintain exclusive access while opening attached tables

If you try to attach a shared database file in a multiuser environment while another user has the file open, you receive a message such as `Can't Open FileName` or `Table TableName is exclusively locked`. Access Version 1.0 needs exclusive use of the file during the attaching process, which occurs each time you open an Access database with an attached file. After Access successfully attaches the file, other users can share the file. Accordingly, you must wait until all other users close the file and then attach it.

Maintain referential integrity in tables with macros or Access Basic

You cannot set default relationships between attached tables or between an attached table and a table in an Access database. To maintain referential integrity when you update attached tables, you must write macros or (preferably) Access Basic code.

In most client-server databases, the server database application includes referential integrity maintenance capabilities. If you are using an attached client-server table *and* a related Access table, however, you must implement referential integrity tests.

Referential integrity requires that you delete all records in a related table that depend on a record you want to delete in a base or primary table. See "Perform cascade deletions with a macro and a query" in Chapter 6 for a tip on deleting dependent records automatically with a macro and "Test for relational integrity with Access Basic code" in Chapter 10 for a tip on peforming cascade deletions with Access Basic.

Referential integrity also requires that all records in a related table have a corresponding record in a base table. In Chapter 5, the tip "Look up data for the 'one' side of a many-to-one query" shows you how to ensure that related records you add each have a corresponding record in the base table.

Change Clipper applications to use index files supported by Access 1.0

If you are using Clipper's native NTX index files, you face problems with them in Access 1.0. Access cannot update NTX files. In Access, you can view but not update DBF files created by Clipper applications, and changes you make to existing data aren't reflected in the NTX file. If you add a new record, you receive an error message when Clipper applications use the file and its associated indexes.

The only available solution in Access 1.0 is to change your Clipper application so that it creates and uses NDX files rather than NTX files. Unfortunately, this change slows your Clipper applications.

Import rather than attach DBF files created by FoxPro 2.x

Access Version 1.0 isn't compatible with attached DBF files created by FoxPro 2.x. You can import all FoxPro DBF files, however.

Attach Btrieve tables by using Xtrieve data dictionary files

Earlier, the tip "Use Xtrieve data dictionary files to import Btrieve tables" shows you how to use Xtrieve data dictionary files to *import* Btrieve tables. You also need Xtrieve DDF files to *attach* Btrieve tables. Altering the DDF files is even more important for attaching files than for importing them.

If you are developing an application, you don't want to use the active Btrieve files for test purposes. Instead, copy the Xtrieve databases DDF and DAT files to another location, such as your hard disk.

If you are using fully qualified (well-formed) or universal naming conventions (UNC), the path data contained in FILES.DDF is invalid for the copies. In this situation, you must make a new FILES.DDF file for your copied DAT files or modify a copy of the FILES.DDF file to change the path. If FILES.DDF contains specifications for the file name but not the path, you can copy the DAT and DDF files to your

\ACCESS directory. You can attach the tables, as long as \ACCESS remains the current directory.

Note: Don't open any files in another directory; otherwise, you change the current directory.

Redefine problem Btrieve indexes for importing into Access

Btrieve tables can contain indexes that are less than or greater than the width of a single field, but you cannot use such indexes in Xtrieve databases. (Xtrieve ignores these indexes.) Btrieve indexes with specified widths other than that of the field from which they are created cause Access to issue the message `TableName is corrupted or isn't a Microsoft Access database`. The import operation ends when you choose OK. To import such a table, you must redefine the indexes so that each index is the width of the field. If you need a composite index, specify a multiple-segment index comprised of two indexes, each with the length of the individual field.

Add more SQL connections to ensure SQL Server support

Most client-server data access applications (usually called *front-ends*) process one operation, such as a request to process a query, at a time. Such an application requires only one server connection while the process is executing. With Access, however, you can have many queries open at one time. If your form is based on a query and you have three combo boxes whose row source property is based on queries, for example, you need four connections to the server while the form is open. If you run out of client connections, you receive a cryptic ODBC error message, such as [`-8008`], with no text description of the error.

To avoid this problem, have your database administrator increase the number of connections to SQL Server, or other client-server databases, from which you attach tables using the ODBC Administrator. This way, the server can support all users of the Access applications.

5

Making the Most of Queries

This chapter is devoted to tips to make your select and action queries more effective. Access's graphical query by example (QBE) methodology simplifies the query design process by extensive use of drag-and-drop procedures. Nevertheless, to fill in the cells of the query design grid, you need to understand how Access processes queries. You also need a working knowledge of Access's operators and expressions to design effective queries. Que's *Using Access for Windows*, Special Edition, has an entire chapter devoted to Access's operators, functions, and expressions.

Use expressions to sort queries on any part of a text field

Use the Mid() function to sort on any character or group of characters in a text field of a table. Suppose that you use part numbers such as 100-233-421-A. To create a calculated query column Expr1 that sorts by the alphabetic suffix, enter

Mid ([Part Number],13,1)

in the field row of the query design grid. The suffix is the 13th character in the Part Number field and is one character long.

When you enter the `Mid()` function, Access adds `Expr1:` as the name of the query column. Add an ascending sort to the column and click the show check box, if you don't want to display the calculated field in your query.

Learn SQL while you create queries

Access's graphical query by example (QBE) window creates the standard query language (SQL) statements most applications use. To see the translation of your query design to an SQL statement, after you create your query in Design mode, choose SQL from the View menu to display the SQL statement Access creates for you. An understanding of the syntax of SQL is very helpful when you use queries to populate combo boxes on forms or write Access Basic code.

Create sub-queries with Access filters

When you apply a filter to a query result, you create a sub-query; the filter specification is added to the Criteria row. You can use query results, as well as tables, as the data source for queries.

To create a sub-query from a query open in Run or Design mode, click the New Query toolbar button. (You need to save the query before you can use the query as the basis of a sub-query.) A field list window for the source query appears in the query design pane. Query columns that correspond to key field(s) of underlying tables aren't displayed in boldface type, and default relationships don't create joins between primary and foreign keys automatically, as occurs when you join tables. You can add tables or other queries, however, and create joins between your query and other tables or queries on corresponding key fields, just as you can with tables.

Note: Access doesn't support sub-queries (also called *nested queries*) contained within a query. In ANSI SQL, you can include a SELECT statement in a WHERE clause to create sub-queries. You need to create a separate Access sub-query to emulate the nested sub-query capability of ANSI SQL. Access doesn't support the SQL UNION operator that combines the results of two queries into one.

Use LEFT JOINs to include all base table records

When you use the default INNER JOIN of Access queries, values for selected fields of the base table appear only when one or more corresponding records are found in a related table. In many cases, you want to display information for all base table records, regardless of whether a related record exists.

If you have a Customers base table and an Invoices related table, for example, you likely would add name and address information for a new customer before an invoice is issued to that customer. To create a LEFT JOIN that includes all records in the base table, follow these steps:

1. Add the base table to the query, and then add the related table.

2. Drag the fields you want to include in the query to the query design grid.

3. Double-click the join line between the two tables, or choose Query Join Properties. The Join Properties choice is disabled (grayed) until you select a join line with a single mouse click.

4. Choose option 2 from the Query Properties dialog that displays all records in the base table. This action

creates a LEFT JOIN, indicated by an arrow pointing from the left to the right, added to the join line.

5. Run the query. Base table records without related table records are indicated by Null values in the columns for fields of the related table.

If you want to display only those customers for whom no invoices have been entered, add the **Is Null** criteria to one of the columns that represents fields from the Invoices table.

Note: Whether you use a LEFT JOIN or a RIGHT JOIN to display all one-side records in a one-to-many relationship (regardless of the existence of a record on the many side) depends on the relationship between the tables as they appear in your query design. Traditionally, the one side of the query is the leftmost table in a QBE design. If you place the many-side table to the left of the one-side table, you need to use a RIGHT JOIN.

Look up data for the "one" side of a many-to-one query

Access has a unique capability to add data automatically for the "one" side of a many-to-one outer join query. Microsoft calls this technique *row fix-up*. Access's query dynasets enable you to add new records to the many side of a query based on a many-to-one relationship, but not to the one side. If you design your query for the row fix-up method and add a new record to the many side of the many-to-one relationship, Access adds the data for the one side.

Try the row fix-up technique for yourself:

1. Create a new query, and add the Products and Categories tables of NWIND.MDB to it, with the Products table to the left. Access automatically creates the join between the Category ID fields of the

two tables because the Products table has a default relationship to the Categories table.

2. Create a RIGHT JOIN between the Category ID of the two tables to display all records in the Products table and only those records in the Categories table with Category IDs that match records in the Products table. (To do so, double-click the join line and then click option 3 in the Join Properties dialog.)

3. Add the Product ID, Product Name, and Category ID fields from the Products table and the Category Name and Description fields of the Categories table to the query. (Make sure that the Category ID field you add is from the Products table, not the Categories table.) The query should appear as shown in figure 5.1.

4. Run the query to view the result.

5. Add a new product, such as **Evan Evans Bevan Lager**, to the query. When you enter a valid Category ID value, such as **BEVR**, Access looks up the BEVR record in the Categories table and adds the values of the Category Name and Description in these query columns.

6. Save the query as **Row Fix-Up Query**.

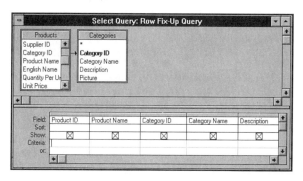

Fig. 5.1 *The design of a row fix-up query.*

Note: This tip is based on article Q95048, "Use Row Fix-up Technique to Look Up Info Automatically," from the Microsoft Knowledge Base (GO MSKB) on CompuServe. To use this query in conjunction with a combo box on a form, see the tip "Use forms based on row fix-up queries to look up data" in Chapter 7, "Designing Optimal Forms."

Use RIGHT JOINs to delete orphan records in related tables

 Referential integrity requires that all records in a related table have a corresponding record in a base table. Records in a related table that don't meet this test are called *orphan* records. If you have orphan records in a related table, Access doesn't let you take advantage of its automatic maintenance of referential integrity feature.

To identify orphan records for deletion, follow these steps to create a RIGHT JOIN on the primary key of the base table and the corresponding foreign key of the related table:

1. Add the base table to the query and then add the related table.

2. Drag the primary key field of the base table to the first query column and the corresponding foreign key field of the related table to the second column.

3. Create a join between the primary and foreign key fields, if a join is not created for you automatically. Double-click the join line between the two tables or choose **Q**uery Join Properties to display the Join Properties dialog.

4. Choose option 3 to display all records in the related table. This action adds to the join line a RIGHT JOIN, indicated by an arrow pointing from the right to the

left. Choose SQL from the View menu to verify that RIGHT JOIN appears in the SQL statement Access creates from your query design.

5. Run the query. Orphan records don't display a value in column one of the resulting query.

6. Select the orphan records with the record select buttons, and then press Delete to remove them from the related table.

Use the SQL WHERE clause to accomplish conventional equijoins

You can create a conventional equijoin (equivalent to an INNER JOIN in Access SQL) with the SQL WHERE clause. Consider the following SQL statement:

```
SELECT Table1.Field1, Table2.Field1 FROM Table1, Table2
WHERE Table1.Field1 = Table2.Field1;
```

It creates an INNER JOIN on Field1 of Table1 and Table2. When you view queries in Access's graphical QBE, joins created with the WHERE clause aren't indicated by join lines between the fields. When you write Access Basic code to create SQL statements for queries, using the WHERE clause rather than JOIN statements to create equi-joins makes the code simpler.

Use parentheses to specify numeric values in query criteria for text fields

 With Access, you can use arithmetic operators in WHERE clause expressions of queries, even for columns whose field data type is Text. Arithmetic operators may be useful with postal code fields, for example, which usually are set up as text fields to accommodate the alphanumeric codes used in Canada and the

UK (WX1 5LT), as well as Europe and Scandinavia (S-10320 in Sweden). You can use arithmetic operators because the Text data type is really a Variant data type of sub-type 8 (String).

To find only the records of customers with postal codes of 90000 and above, follow these steps:

1. Create a new query and add Northwind Traders' Customers table.

2. Drag the Customer Name, Postal Code, and Country fields to the query design grid.

3. Enter >=**90000** in the Criteria column of the Postal Code column. (Access alters your expression to >=`"90000"` because the field data type is Text.)

4. Run the query. Records for Postal Codes greater than 90000 and Postal Codes beginning with letters are returned, because >="90000" compares the ANSI value of the text field, not the numeric value. The letters have a higher value than numbers in the ANSI sort order.

5. Change the expression in the Criteria column to **Val([Postal Code])>=(90000)**. The `Val()` function converts strings that begin with a number to the numeric value. The parentheses are needed to fix 90000 as a numeric value. If you omit the parentheses, Access adds quotes around 90000 and you receive a type mismatch error.

6. Run the query. The query returns what you wanted—only records with postal codes 90000 and above.

7. Change the expression to **Between 90000 And 94999**. Access changes the expression to `Between "90000"` `And "94999"`.

8. Run the query. Notice that quoted values work with the Between … And operator. (Entering **Between (90000) and (94999)** results in a Type mismatch error message.)

If you write complex functions for criteria, such as **Val(Mid([Postal Code],2,3)) >= (200)**, add the parentheses shown around the 200. Otherwise, Access surrounds 200 with quotation marks and displays a Type mismatch error message when you run the query.

Use DISTINCT and DISTINCTROW to avoid duplicate field values

ANSI-standard SQL specifies that the DISTINCT qualifier added to a Select query causes rows that have duplicate information in the selected fields to appear only once in the query result. Access SQL adds the nonstandard DISTINCTROW qualifier. DISTINCTROW requires that all field values of records in a table, not just the values of fields included in your query, be identical to eliminate the return of duplicate records.

If you don't include DISTINCT or DISTINCTROW after the SELECT keyword, the query returns all records that fit the specified Criteria, regardless of duplicate field values. Omitting either qualifier is the same as adding SQL's ALL qualifier to the statement. Removing the default mark from the Restrict Available Fields check box in the Query Properties dialog has the same effect as adding the SQL ALL qualifier to SELECT queries.

A minor advantage of the DISTINCTROW qualifier is that with it you can edit fields on the one side of a one-to-many relationship, but only if you don't include any fields from the many side in your query.

Use SQL aggregate functions to return totals and averages

SQL aggregate functions return totals, average values, and record counts for queries. To use the SQL aggregate functions, follow these steps:

1. Add the Totals row to your query grid by clicking the Totals toolbar button (with the S or summation sign), or by choosing View Totals.

2. Add the table(s) to the query.

3. Drag the fields that you want to total, average, or count to the query design grid.

4. Select the aggregate function to use from the Totals combo box for each field.

Create subtotals for groups of records

To create subtotals for groups of records, do the following in addition to what you did in the preceding tip:

1. Add the field on which to base the grouping.

2. Select Group By from the Totals combo box.

3. Enter the expression to group by in the criteria field.

If you want to summarize orders received on each day in March 1993, for example, enter **Like "3/*/93"** in the Criteria row of the Group By column. If you use the Northwind Traders sample database to try the preceding steps, substitute 92 for 93; otherwise, the query won't return any records.

Use calculated fields to group by special criteria

Use calculated fields to create special grouping criteria beyond the capability of the Like operator. To summarize orders by month, using the Northwind Traders sample database, follow these steps:

1. Enter **Month:Month**([**Order Date**]) in the Field row of a blank query column.

2. Choose Group By from the Totals combo box for this column.

3. Restrict the values to a single year by adding a column for the Order Date field.

4. Choose Where from the Totals combo box.

5. Enter **Between #1/1/92# And #12/31/92#** in the Criteria row.

Use SQL aggregate queries to create summary tables

Queries you design by using SQL aggregate functions and calculated group-by fields are similar to crosstab queries. In fact, you can use a crosstab query rather than the select query described in the preceding tip to accomplish the same result. You also can convert "totals" queries to make table or append queries. You cannot use a crosstab query, however, to create a new summary table or append records to a summary table. You can, however, base a make table or an append query on a crosstab query.

Note: Creating tables to store data you can create with queries against existing tables isn't a good database practice; doing so violates the no-duplicate-data rule. If, however, you need to display historical data quickly or purge detail records from tables after a given period of time, keeping historical summary tables may be warranted.

Use different prompts when you have more than one parameter

Parameter queries often require that you enter two parameters—for example, beginning and ending dates. Make sure that you differentiate the prompts for each parameter you need for the query. Otherwise, if you assign the same prompt to two parameters, as with the criteria **Between [Enter Date:] And [Enter Date:]**, Access interprets both parameters as a single parameter. As a result, you never see the dialog for the second parameter.

Use fixed column headings to keep monthly crosstab queries in order

You may be tempted to avoid entering fixed column headings in crosstab queries that show distribution of values by month. Whether you specify three-letter abbreviations or full month names as column headings, the columns display in alphabetical order (Apr, Aug, Dec, and so on), not date sequence (Jan, Feb, Mar, and so on). To enter fixed column headings, choose View Query Properties and enter the month names or abbreviations in sequence, separated by commas or semicolons.

Fixed column headings also speed the operation of crosstab queries by making better use of Access's query optimizer. An additional benefit of fixed column headings is that columns for months without data appear in your query.

Use indexes to speed most—but not all—queries

Add indexes to fields of tables on which you base queries. Indexes on foreign key fields speed the joining process. (Access automatically creates an index on the primary key field.) Access uses a process called *query optimization* that uses the indexes you have created, if these indexes correspond to fields participating in a join, sort orders, or filter criteria. Query optimization greatly improves the performance of joins on tables with a large number of records.

Don't add to tables indexes you don't need or Access can't use. The more indexes you add, the slower editing and appending new records becomes. Access doesn't use indexes to optimize queries with the following types of criteria:

- `Like` expressions with a preceding `*` wild card, such as `Like "*abc"`

- Complex expressions using the OR operator (multiple criteria entered in more than one criteria row of the query grid)

Use expressions to help build criteria to search for words

Using a criteria expression such as **Like "The *"** returns words such as *Theater, Thesaurus,* and *The quick brown fox* because Access strips spaces that precede and follow wild cards in `Like` expressions (`Like "The *"` becomes `Like "The*"`). Substitute the expression **Like "The*" And Mid(FieldName,4,1) = " "** to specify the requirement for a space character in a `Like` criteria of this type.

Preserve data by backing up tables before you run action queries on them

Action queries make permanent changes in your table data. Before you use an action query to update or append records to a table, create a backup copy of the table to use in case something goes wrong with your action query. You can create a backup copy of a table by copying the table to the Clipboard, and then pasting it to a temporary table with a new name.

To copy a table, do the following:

1. Make the Database window active.

2. Select the table from the Table list.

3. Press Ctrl+C to copy the table to the Clipboard.

4. Press Ctrl+V to display the Paste Table As dialog.

5. Enter the temporary table name in the Table Name text box.

6. Choose OK to create the backup copy.

Use delete and append queries to update tables

Maintaining data in Access tables often involves imported files that contain changes to existing records in the table and new records that you need to add. Updating membership rosters and mailing lists with tables imported from text or worksheet files are typical examples. Assuming that your base table and the imported table have a unique primary key, you can use delete and append queries to create an updated table. Follow these steps:

1. Use a delete query to remove the records in the base table that correspond to update records in the imported table.

2. Create an append query to append all records from the imported table.

Use an update query to create unique primary keys

Data you import from worksheet and text files seldom include a primary key field. You can use a calculated value column to an action query to create a primary key field for existing tables, as well as action queries used to update or append records to tables.

You may find that creating meaningful, unique primary key fields for certain types of data, such as mailing lists that must be updated periodically from imported data, is challenging. Try using a combination of several letters of the last name, combined with the first few characters of the address. This type of key often is used to identify magazine subscribers.

Use an SQL aggregate query to delete duplicate values

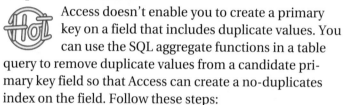

Access doesn't enable you to create a primary key on a field that includes duplicate values. You can use the SQL aggregate functions in a table query to remove duplicate values from a candidate primary key field so that Access can create a no-duplicates index on the field. Follow these steps:

1. Create a query based on the table, and add all fields of the table to the query.

2. Click the Totals toolbar button or choose View Totals.

3. Select Group By from the Totals combo box in the column of the candidate key field.

4. Select First (one of the SQL aggregate functions) from the Totals combo box for all other columns.

5. Choose Query Make Table and assign the table a new name in the Query Properties dialog.

6. Click the Run Query toolbar button to create the no-duplicates table.

7. Add the primary key to your new table in Table Design mode.

This query has the same effect as creating a copy of an indexed xBase table with SET UNIQUE ON; only the first record with the duplicate key is included in the query result. See document Q90809 in the Microsoft Knowledge Base, "How to Use a Query to Filter Unique Data," for an example of this type of query.

Use macros to solve validation rule problems while updating with queries

When you use update or append queries to edit or add records to a table, table validation rules aren't enforced. Access only checks to determine whether the field data types of the source update or append data match the corresponding fields of the target table. In most cases, you can add criteria to your action query so that rows violating domain integrity aren't included in the query result.

If you cannot use query criteria to maintain domain integrity, use a validation macro to verify that the data in the target table follows the rules. Chapter 6 discusses tips for creating validation macros.

Remove indexes before deleting many records from a table

When you use a delete query to remove a large number of records from a table that has one or more indexes, the deletion process can be very slow, even on a fast computer. The slowdown is because Access updates the index(es) for each deletion. For large bulk deletes, removing the indexes (and the primary key fields, because primary keys have indexes, too) and then running the delete query is usually faster.

Note: Remember to add the primary key and rebuild other indexes after the bulk delete.

6

Using Macros Effectively

Access macros bring to you the event-oriented programming techniques that all Windows applications use. In Access, macros comprise one or more *actions* that respond to *events* that occur when a user clicks a command button, opens or closes a form, or enters a value in a control object. You choose the action you want to occur from a combo box list in the Actions column of the macro design window.

Microsoft advertises Access as a relational database management system (RDBMS) that doesn't require that you learn a programming language. In reality, however, Access macros are programs in disguise. You can use If expressions to determine whether a macro action is to execute. You even can create loops with the RunMacro action.

Fortunately, Access has only 42 macro actions from which to choose, which makes learning its macro programming language much easier than mastering Access Basic, which has several hundred keywords. The vast majority of the applications you create with Access require little or no Access Basic code.

Most books about Access discuss macros after covering forms and reports. Because you seldom—if ever—will create a form that doesn't use macros, this chapter of tips on using macros appears before the chapter with tips on creating forms and reports.

Substitute command buttons and macro actions for menu choices

Character-based (DOS) database applications tradition- ally use a series of menus that lead to submenus and fi- nally display a data entry form or print a report. Users make menu choices by pressing a number or a letter key. By contrast, Windows applications usually substitute command buttons for menu choices, although you can create your own drop-down menus to supplement or take the place of command buttons. You attach a named macro to each button that performs the chosen action, such as opening a form or printing a report.

The OnPush event of each of the seven command buttons of the Forms Switchboard form (shown in fig. 6.1) is at- tached to one of the macros contained in the Forms Switchboard Buttons macrogroup, shown in figure 6.2.

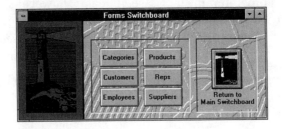

Fig. 6.1 *Using command buttons to replace menu choices.*

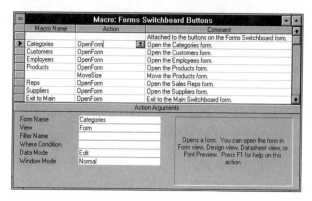

Fig. 6.2 *The macrogroup that responds to the command buttons of figure 6.1.*

Store related macros in macrogroups

The Forms Switchboard in figure 6.1 has seven buttons. If you create a separate macro to respond to each event that originates from your forms and reports, the macro list in your database window will become unmanageable.

In Access, you can place as many macros as you want in a single macro object called a *macrogroup*. To create a macrogroup for each form and report of your application, follow these steps:

1. Click the View Macro Names toolbar button (the button with "xyz" at the top), or choose View Macro Names in Macro Design mode.

2. Assign each macro its own name in the Macro Name column.

To run a macro contained in a macrogroup, enter the name of the macrogroup object, a period, and the name of the macro as the value of the event (OnPush, for instance) in the Properties window of the control object (a command button) on your form. To run the Categories macro of the Forms Switchboard Buttons macrogroup, for example, enter **Forms Switchboard Buttons.Categories** as the value of the OnPush property for the Categories button.

Drag-and-drop a macro to create a command button

By using the drag-and-drop features built into Access, you can create command buttons from the macros you write. Follow these steps:

1. Give the Database window the focus.

2. Click the name of the macro to which the new command button is to be attached.

3. Drag the macro's icon to the location in the form where you want the command button that runs the macro, and drop it there.

Note: Click-and-drag techniques for creating command buttons don't apply to macros contained in macrogroups, unless the macro you want to attach is the first macro in the group. If you omit the macro name and attach the name of a macrogroup only to an event, the first member of the macrogroup is executed.

Speed form and report design by keeping macro names short

Use short names for macros and especially for macro-group objects. Typing **FSB.***MacroName* instead of **Forms Switchboard Buttons.***MacroName* saves about 150 keystrokes, if you have seven buttons on your form.

You also can add a descriptive comment as the first line of the macro to describe what FSB means. Enter your first macro action on the next line so that you can add a separate comment, if required, for the action.

Add Alt+*key* designations to your command buttons

Add hot key designations to each option button to give users the option of clicking the command button or pressing Alt plus the underlined letter. To do so, add an ampersand (&) in front of the letter of the Caption text that you want to assign as the hot key for the choice. Enter **Ca&tegories**, for example, to assign Alt+T to the Categories button. Access adds an underline to the button's hot key in Form Run mode.

Note: Make sure that you choose a unique letter as the Alt+key combination for each button.

Use labels to explain button pictures

Command buttons with pictures as captions are pretty, but they don't always explain the purpose of the button. Because a picture replaces the Caption text of a button, you need a label below the button to explain its function, as shown for the Return to Main Switchboard button of figure 6.1.

Use the Caption property of picture buttons to add Alt+*key* combinations

Even if the bit map you apply to picture buttons hides the Caption text, you can assign an Alt+*key* combination to a picture. First, enter & and the letter as the Caption text for your picture button. Then add an ampersand in front of the same letter in the label for your button to indicate the Alt+*key* choice.

Start an Access application with an AutoExec macro

Users of commercial database applications expect the main menu to appear when they launch the application.

You can accomplish the same result with an AutoExec macro.

Access reserves the name AutoExec for a macro that runs when you open an Access database. As an example, to hide the NWIND.MDB database window and open the Main Switchboard form automatically when you open NWIND.MDB, create an AutoExec macro with the following actions:

Action	Argument	Value
DoMenuItem	Menu Bar	Form
	Menu Name	Window
	Command	Hide
OpenForm	Form Name	**Main Switchboard**
	View	Form
	Data Mode	Edit
	Window Mode	Normal

Note: The examples of macro code given in this book don't show macro arguments that you leave blank. Values of arguments you enter from the keyboard are shown in **boldface** type; those you select from combo box lists are shown in regular type.

Save the macrogroup with the name **AutoExec**. Close NWIND.MDB and then reopen it. The Database window disappears (the Hide command applies to the window with the focus), and the Main Switchboard form appears. Choose Window Show to display the Show Window dialog and then double-click Database: NWIND to make the Database window visible again.

Hold down the Shift key to stop the AutoExec macro

To prevent the AutoExec macro from running, hold down the Shift key when you click a recently opened database file name (such as NWIND.MDB from the File menu) or when you double-click a file name in the Open Database dialog. If you hold the Shift key down when you double-click Access's icon, Access opens minimized to an icon. If you continue to hold the Shift key down while Access is loading, Access doesn't run your AutoExec macro. Double-click the Access icon to restore the window of your application, and then choose a database to open.

Use SendKeys to maximize forms

Maximized mode isn't an option for the Window argument of the OpenForm macro action. If you want to open a form in Maximized mode, add the SendKeys action to the bottom of your AutoExec macro to send Alt+hyphen (-) and then X to the Document Control menu of your form, as follows:

Action	Argument	Value
SendKeys	Keystrokes	%-X
	Wait	No

Temporarily disable a macro with the False condition

To inhibit operation of an AutoExec macro or any other macro you want to prevent from running, add a condition to the macro actions that cannot occur, such as False. The following example macro is disabled with the False condition:

Condition	Action	Argument	Value
False	DoMenuItem	Menu Bar	Form
		Menu Name	Window
		Command	Hide
...	OpenForm	Form Name	**Main Switchboard**
		View	Form
		Data Mode	Edit
		Window Mode	Normal

Note: The ellipsis (...) preceding the OpenForm action indicates that the condition applies to this action as well as to the DoMenuItem action.

Disable long macros with the StopMacro action

If a large number of actions exist in the macro that you want to inhibit, insert a conditional StopMacro in the first line of your macro, and use the reverse logic:

Condition	Action	Argument	Value
True	StopMacro		
	DoMenuItem	Menu Bar	Form
		Menu Name	Window
		Command	Hide
	OpenForm	Form Name	**Main Switchboard**
		View	Form
		Data Mode	Edit
		Window Mode	Normal

Disabling macros often is useful when you are debugging macros that call other macros with the RunMacro action.

Add the True condition to remind yourself that the StopMacro line is temporary. You then can reenable the macro by setting the condition for StopMacro to False.

Run selected macros from the Access command line

To customize how an application runs for individual users, specify a macro (other than AutoExec) to run when the users open the database. Enter the name of the database to open, followed by /X and the macro's name.

If some users want to go directly to the Forms Switchboard when they launch Access, for example, change the name of the AutoExec macro to **OpenFSB**. Then change the value of the Form Name argument of the OpenForm action of OpenFSB to **Forms Switchboard**. Enter **msaccess.exe nwind.mdb /X OpenFSB** in the Command Line text box in the application's Program Item Properties dialog for the user's Access icon.

Note: If you use a command-line parameter to execute a specified macro, make sure that you don't have an AutoExec macro in your database. If you don't delete or rename the AutoExec macro, it runs first; then the command-line macro runs.

Imitate labels with unbound text boxes and GoToControl actions

To create a label whose text changes depending on the state of an application, substitute an unbound text box without an attached label. Follow these steps:

1. Set the text box's Border and Fill properties to clear (the defaults for labels) with the Palette.

2. Use the SetValue action to enter the content (caption) of the text box. Unlike a label, the text box will receive the focus at some time during data entry, depending on the text box's sequence in the Tab Order you set.

3. To prevent the text box *cum* label from receiving the focus for more than an instant, add a new macro to the macrogroup for your form that uses the GoToControl action to pass the focus to another control. (You cannot use 0 or –1 to prevent a text box from appearing in the Tab Order and thus receiving the focus at some point.)

4. Attach the new macro to the OnEnter event of the control, which occurs when the text box receives the focus. The text box loses the focus a split second after it receives the focus.

Change the Caption property of a command button

The Caption property of command buttons is read-only in Run mode. The only way you can change the Caption property of a command button is to create two superimposed buttons, each with a different caption, as follows:

1. Create two command buttons of the same size, each with the caption you want.

2. Place one button over the other on the form.

3. Add two macros to the macrogroup for the form: one that shows the bottom button and hides the top one, and one that does the reverse.

The following example macrogroup alternates display of two buttons, Btn1 and Btn2.

Macro Name	Action	Argument	Value
ShowBtn1	SetValue	Btn2.Visible	No
	SetValue	Btn1.Visible	Yes
ShowBtn2	SetValue	Btn1.Visible	No
	SetValue	Btn2.Visible	Yes

Note: When a button's Visible property is No, its Enabled property is implicitly set to No; you don't need to set the Enabled property of an invisible button to No. Access sets the property for you.

You can use the same hide-and-show technique to alter the captions of other control objects, such as option buttons and check boxes.

Document macros with Database Analyzer

One reason database developers use Access Basic code rather than macros is documentation. You can print Access Basic code to document your application, but Access doesn't include a built-in feature that enables you to print out the actions, arguments, conditions, and values that comprise Access macros. You can use, however, the Database Analyzer library (ANALYZER.MDA) supplied with Access to create a table, similar to the one shown in figure 6.3, that includes a record for each action in your macrogroup.

You can create a report from the table that displays the macros in a format similar to that used in this chapter. Tips on installing and using the Database Analyzer are included in Chapter 12, "Taking Advantage of Libraries and Wizards."

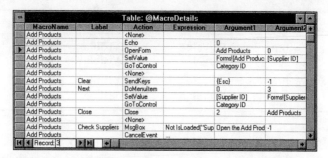

Fig. 6.3   *The @MacroDetails table created by Database Analyzer from NWIND.MDB's AddProducts macro.*

Debug Access macros with the Macro Single Step dialog

If your macro doesn't perform as expected, click the Single Step toolbar button (with the footprint) and initiate an event that runs the macro. The Macro Single Step dialog appears when the event calls the first macro action. (The action shown in fig. 6.4 is the third record, shown selected, in fig. 6.3.)

Fig. 6.4   *The Macro Single Step dialog.*

Use the Macro Single Step dialog to debug your macro. Click the Step button to proceed to the next action or the Continue button to execute the balance of your macro without interruption. Clicking the Halt button has the same effect as the StopMacro action. Single-step mode applies to the operation of all macros until you turn it off.

Replicate groups of macro actions with the Clipboard

If you are writing a macro that consists of similar sets of actions that apply to different control objects, you can save time by using the Clipboard to create duplicates. Here's how:

1. Select the set of actions you want to replicate by clicking the selection button of first action and then dragging the mouse to include the remaining actions in the selection.

2. Press Ctrl+C to copy the selection to the Clipboard.

3. Click a selection button on a blank row where you want to start the new macro.

   Note: To add a blank row, select the row above which you want the blank line to appear, and then press Insert.

4. Press Ctrl+V to paste the selection to your macro-group.

5. Edit the Macro Name and the values for arguments of the actions as necessary.

Note: When you copy or cut a set of macro actions to the Clipboard, blank lines used to format your macrogroup to make it more readable are lost. You need to reinsert the blank lines by selecting the line below which the blank line is desired and then pressing Insert.

Enforce domain integrity with validation macros

Validation rules added as methods to tables aren't enforced unless the field is updated during data entry. If you establish a table-level validation rule that requires an entry in the Last Name field (Is Not Null), for example, the Last Name entry isn't tested if you use the Enter, Tab, or arrow key to skip the entry in the field. In this case, Access considers that the data in the text box isn't updated (no change occurred).

Create a validation macro, similar to the following example, attached to the OnExit event of a text box bound to the Last Name field to prevent skipping the entry and leaving a blank field.

Macro Name	Condition	Action	Argument	Value
Test Last	IsNull ([Last Name])	MsgBox	Message	*Message*
			Beep	Yes
			Type	Warning!
			Title	*Title*
	...	CancelEvent		

The ellipsis (...) in the Condition column indicates that the **IsNull( )** condition applies to all macro actions. Substitute an appropriate message and title for your message box for *Message* and *Title*. The CancelEvent action prevents the attempted move to the next field of the form until the condition function returns False.

Note: You don't need to test for null values in the primary key field or a field that's a component of a composite primary key field. Access displays a "nocando" message box when you try to update a record with a Null value in a key field. Intercepting the error at the point of entry and displaying your own, more specific message box, however, is a better practice.

Use a macro to enforce validation of all critical fields

The field-by-field validation procedure described in the preceding tip doesn't ensure domain integrity totally. You can bypass macro validation rules by moving to another record without passing the focus through all the text boxes on the form with the Enter, Tab, or arrow keys. Thus, you need to perform a test on all fields for which domain integrity enforcement is applicable by a macro attached to the BeforeUpdate event of the form. The BeforeUpdate event is triggered when you initiate a move to another record but before Access saves the updated data to the current record.

If you use macros to test each critical field as described in the preceding tip, you can create a new macro comprised of a series of RunMacro actions to reuse the individual macros for the record updating test.

The following example saves repetitious entry of macro actions by reusing the individual validation macros attached to the OnExit event. Attach the Domain Test macro to the BeforeUpdate property of the form.

Macro Name	Action	Argument	Value
Domain Test	RunMacro	Macro Name	*Macro*.Test Last
	RunMacro	Macro Name	*Macro*.Test First
	RunMacro	Macro Name	*Macro*.Test SSN

Note: Add an additional StopAllMacros action to the end of each macro you call with the RunMacro action. StopAllMacros ends operation of the Domain Test macro when a domain integrity violation occurs.

Create Yes/No message boxes with a MsgBox() condition

The MsgBox macro action can create only an information message box with an OK button. Access macros provide no way to respond to use of the Esc key to indicate the "Not OK" condition. To make a choice between performing and not performing an action with a message box, use the MsgBox() function as a condition for your macro. To require confirmation of deletion of a record, for example, create a macro similar to the following:

Macro Name	Condition	Action
Confirm Delete	MsgBox("*Msg*", *Type*, "*Title*") <> *YesValue*	CancelEvent

Substitute your message (such as "Do you want to delete this record?") for *Msg* and the title bar text you want for *Title*. Substitute the combined value of the type of message box (number and captions of buttons), and the icon you want to appear for *Type*. *YesValue* depends on the *Type* you select; if *Type* = 36, *YesValue* (the value returned when you click the Yes button) = 6. A value of 36 provides Yes and No buttons and the ? icon. Search Help for MsgBox for other choices.

Use a macro to test for referential integrity violations

Access tests for violations of referential integrity, if you establish default relations between two tables in the Relationships dialog and mark the Enforce Referential Integrity check box for the relationship. Access doesn't test for violations of referential integrity until you try to save the changes to the record.

Testing for referential integrity violations before Access performs the test for you is a good practice. This way, you can create your own, more informative message box to advise the operator of the error.

To test for the presence of a primary key value of a base table corresponding to a value entered in a text box that is bound to a foreign key field in a related table, use the domain aggregate function, DCount(), in a macro attached to the OnUpdate or OnExit event of the text box bound to the foreign key field. Here's an example:

Macro Name	Condition	Action	Argument	Value
Test Key	DCount [*Primary Key*], "*Table*", [*Primary Key*] = *FormName.* [*Foreign Key*]) = 0	MsgBox	Message	*Message*
			Beep	Yes
			Type	Warning!
			Title	*Title*
	...	CancelEvent		

Substitute the name of the primary key field of the base table for *Primary Key* in both occurrences, the name of the base table for *Table*, the name of the form for *FormName*, and the name of the text box that supplies the value for the foreign key of the related table (the same as the name of the foreign key field) for *Foreign Key*. The DCount() function returns 1 if it finds the value of the foreign key in the primary key field of the base table, 0 if it doesn't. See the earlier tip "Enforce domain integrity with validation macros" for values of MsgBox arguments.

Note: Qualify the Foreign Key identifier with the name of the form, because the names of bound text boxes and the fields to which they are bound are the same. When you specify an identifier in a domain aggregate function, Access first tests the identifier against field names of tables and then against control names of the current form to find a match.

Use the opposite logic when testing for the presence of records dependent on the primary key value of a record in a base table that you intend to delete. Change the condition in the preceding example to

> DCount([*Primary Key*], "*Table*", [*Primary Key*] = Forms!*FormName*.[*Foreign Key*]) > 0

and attach the macro to the OnDelete event of the form so that the message box appears and the delete is canceled if dependent records exist.

Perform cascade deletions with a macro and a query

To delete a record from a base table on which records in one or more related tables are dependent, delete the dependent records before you delete the record from the base table. Deleting all dependent records in related tables is called a *cascade deletion* or *cascading delete*.

You can delete dependent records with a macro similar to the following example:

Macro Name	Condition	Action	Argument	Value
Cascade Delete	**MsgBox** ("*Msg*", *Type*, "*Title*") <> *YesValue* ...	CancelEvent		
		StopMacro SetWarnings	Warnings On	No
		RunSQL	SQL Statement	*See following*

Note: Using transaction processing to perform cascade deletions is the more accepted method in RDBMS applications. Transaction processing tries to perform a set of updates to the selected records in multiple tables. If every step in the transaction cannot be completed, the transaction is undone (rolled back). You need to write an Access Basic function that includes the `BeginTrans`, `CommitTrans`, or `RollbackTrans` keywords to use transaction processing techniques with Access. The preceding macro is a shortcut that achieves the same effect, but doesn't include the safety features of transaction processing.

The value of the SQL Statement parameter is as follows:

> **DELETE * FROM** [*RelatedTable*] **WHERE** [*Foreign Key*] = Forms![*FormName*]![*Primary Key*];

Don't forget the semicolon that ends all SQL statements in Access.

The substitutions in the SQL Statement value are the same table, field, and form names as those used earlier in the tip "Use a macro to test for referential integrity violations." In this case, however, the form usually is bound to the base table rather than the relation table.

7

Designing Optimal Forms

Forms convert the data in your tables to information meaningful to your Access application's users. Designing forms to optimize the display of information or the speed and accuracy of data entry involves technical and aesthetic considerations. You must add the necessary control objects to accomplish the objective of your form and at the same time create the "look and feel" of your application. This chapter gives you tips on how to design forms and how to make best use of the control objects that you add to forms.

Design forms for the smallest display that will use your forms

Most PCs with VGA adapter cards have 13- or 14-inch (diagonal) displays and use 16-color, 640-by-480-pixel (standard VGA) mode. A large, complex form may look good in 800-by-600 (SVGA) mode on your 17-inch display or in 1024-by-768 (UVGA) mode on your 21-inch or 24-inch display, but be unsatisfactory for display on a 13-inch

VGA or the smaller LCD displays of laptop and notebook computers. As a result, you should design your forms in a way that looks best on the smallest VGA display that will use your forms.

Check the grid spacing if alignment grid dots don't appear in Design mode

The grid dots that you use to align control objects on forms and reports disappear if the GridX or GridY properties of your form are set to a number greater than 16. Some forms created by the FormWizard have GridX and GridY properties set to 64. If resetting the GridX and GridY spacing to a value of 16 or less doesn't display grid dots in Design mode, choose View Grid to turn on the grid dots.

You can determine whether grid dots appear by default by choosing View Options, selecting the Form & Report design category, and setting the value of the Show Grid option to Yes or No.

Substitute command buttons for record selectors to improve navigation

Access ordinarily uses miniature record selector buttons that emulate the controls of a videocassette or audio tape recorder. These buttons, also called *VCR buttons*, save space because they use only a small area of the form. Longtime users of DOS or other Windows applications, however, may be unaccustomed to using VCR buttons. Because you must position the mouse quite accurately to activate the small buttons, consider changing these buttons to larger command buttons.

Substitute First, Next, Prior, and Last command buttons with attached GoToRecord macro actions for the record selectors. To complete the substitution, set the ScrollBars property of the form to Vertical Only or Neither.

Transaction processing forms require additional buttons, such as Add, OK, Cancel, and Delete. (For transaction processing forms, also consider using Alt+*key* combinations, which enable users to keep their hands on the keyboard.) All forms need a Main Form button, or a Quit or Exit button. Position the buttons in a row near the bottom or in a column to the right of your form, to conform to the practice of DOS and other Windows database applications.

Arrange command buttons logically to make navigation easier

 Devise a logical sequence for the arrangement of command buttons used to navigate between records. Try to keep all buttons that relate to moving the record pointer, adding and deleting records, and accepting or rejecting edits to a record in a single row at the bottom of the form or a column at the right of the form. If you place record navigation buttons in a row, add form navigation buttons in a column to distinguish them.

After you establish a standard set of command buttons for navigating records and forms, maintain the same sequence throughout the applications you create. All forms don't require every button, but using a consistent pattern for mouse movements and—especially—Alt+*key* combinations flattens the learning curve for your applications.

Use hierarchical forms to provide detailed information

Drill-down methods use hierarchical design techniques that enable users of decision-support applications to start with summary data and then obtain increasingly detailed levels of data. An example of a form used as the second level in a drill-down decision-support hierarchy is shown in figure 7.1 (from Que's *Using Access for Windows*, Special Edition). The form preceding that shown in figure 7.1 displays a graph of a firm's total year-to-date sales.

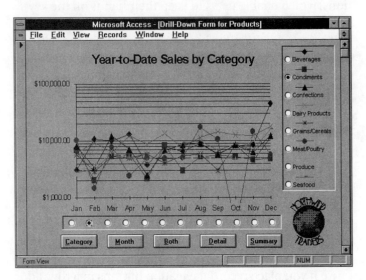

Fig. 7.1 *The second level of a drill-down decision-support form.*

Users select months and categories by clicking option buttons at the bottom of the form. Clicking the Category button activates a form that displays monthly sales for the chosen category. Clicking the Month button leads to a form that shows a pie chart of product sales distribution. Click Both to view the total sales for each product in the chosen category for the selected month. The Detail button brings up a form that offers several other display options. The Summary button returns you to the top level of the hierarchy.

Show and hide forms for better performance

If the computers to run your application have 8M or more of memory, set the Visible property of the form to No to hide rather than close the form. Then, rather than use the OpenForm macro action, set the form's Visible property to Yes. This technique saves the time necessary to load the form from the database file each time you open it.

Showing and hiding forms is particularly effective for decision-support forms that use drill-down techniques, because you may need to refer to values set by control objects (such as an unbound option frame) on a form higher in the hierarchy. A form must be open for you to get the current value of one of the form's control objects for use in a lower-level form.

Use the OnClose event to return the user to another form

You can run a macro that returns the user to another form (such as a switchboard form) when the user closes the current form. To construct this arrangement, attach a macro containing an OpenForm action for the other form to the OnClose event of the current form. (The OnClose event is the only means for trapping the use of the Close choice of the Document Control menu to close a form.)

Don't try to change the design of the current form to which you have added this type of macro, however; clicking the Design toolbar button causes the other form to load rather than the desired result. Wait until you complete the design of your forms before you add an Open-Form action to a macro attached to the OnClose event of another form. (Alternatively, you can add a False condition to the OpenForm action.)

Create modal, modeless, and pop-up windows

Access forms are multiple document interface (MDI) child windows; Access's main window is the parent of the MDI children. The Windows MDI enables you to have as many child windows open at one time as your RAM and temporary or permanent swap file can store.

Modal windows (forms) behave like Windows dialogs; the system disables all other open windows until you close or hide a modal window. Modal windows retain Windows' focus while visible. Use modal windows for purposes such as lookup lists.

Normal MDI child windows are *modeless* windows, which means that you can change the focus to another window while the modeless window is open. Use modeless windows when you want to let the user choose an open window by clicking its surface. Set the Modal property of a form to Yes to create a modal window or No (the default) to make the window modeless.

Pop-up windows remain in front of other modeless windows (an arrangement called *always on top*) until you close them. Pop-up windows are usually small so that you can move them from regions of the form in which you are entering data. Although you can move pop-up windows, you cannot minimize or maximize them, nor can you change the size of pop-up windows by dragging their borders. Use pop-up windows to create floating toolbars or small switchboard forms. To create a pop-up window, set the PopUp property of the form to Yes.

Note: Modal pop-up windows are Windows dialogs, the most common type of modal window. Although the pop-up window retains the focus until you close or hide the window, you can open other dialogs from a modal pop-up form. You need to close each dialog in sequence to return to your original window. To create a dialog, set the Modal and PopUp properties of the form to Yes. Always include an OK or Close button on modal pop-up forms and assign Yes to the value of this button's Default property.

When you change the value of the Modal and PopUp properties of a form from No to Yes and then switch to Form Run mode, the form appears as a normal MDI child window, not a dialog. You need to close the form and then open the form in Form Run mode to make the change in window mode occur.

Use full-screen rather than modeless forms in applications

As a rule, DOS applications don't use multiple modeless forms in overlapping MDI child windows (Borland's SideKick TSR application notwithstanding). DOS users are unaccustomed to choosing from a collection of simultaneously open forms, whether by clicking a form's exposed surface or choosing the form from a drop-down menu. Instead, use full-screen forms in applications you create for others to use, with pop-up windows to assist in making entries or for performing tasks similar to those of Windows common dialogs.

Use dialogs to add or edit records that underlie a form

Substitute modal pop-up forms for subforms when you have limited space available on a main form. Because modal pop-up forms resemble the dialogs of DOS RDBMS applications, DOS users can work comfortably with them.

You can synchronize forms by using the FindRecord macro action as a substitute to the LinkChildFields and LinkMasterFields properties of a subform. Use pop-up forms to add new records to the "many" side of a one-to-many relation when the parent form is based on records in the table on the "one" side.

The form design shown in figure 7.2 is a good candidate for a modal pop-up. You can use modal pop-up forms to add new products, customer contacts, and other records to the "many" side of a many-to-one query that underlies the modal pop-up form.

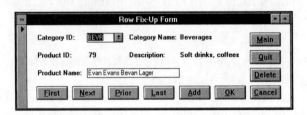

Fig. 7.2 *A form based on a row fix-up query.*

Use forms based on row fix-up queries to look up data

You can look up and display the data from the "one" side of a many-to-one query by using the row fix-up query design described in Chapter 5. Figure 7.2 shows a form based on Chapter 5's row fix-up query that you use to test the use of row fix-up.

To create a form similar to that shown in figure 7.2, follow these steps:

1. Create a new form based on the row fix-up query. Retain the horizontal scroll bar so that the record selectors appear. (You don't need to add the command buttons shown in fig. 7.2.)

2. Drag the Product ID, Product Name, Category Name, and Description fields to the positions shown in figure 7.2.

3. Use the Toolbox to add a combo box bound to the Category ID field of the query. (Click the combo box tool; then click and drag the Category ID field from the Field List window to the form to create the bound combo box.)

4. Set the combo box's RowSource property to the Categories table. Use the default values for the remaining properties of the combo box.

5. Change to Form Run mode, add a new record, and enter a value for the Product Name field.

6. Select the Category ID for the new product from combo box. The row fix-up query fills in the Category name and Description text boxes automatically.

For the query on which this example form is based, see the tip "Look up data for the 'one' side of a many-to-one query" in Chapter 5, "Making the Most of Queries."

Avoid minimizing pop-up forms with macro actions

Access enables you to open a pop-up form minimized to an icon (Window Mode=Icon) or minimize a pop-up form with the Minimize action. Access pop-up forms, however, don't have a Minimize choice in the Document Control menu. Windows 3.x doesn't recognize double-clicking the icon of a minimized window that has no Minimize choice.

In most cases, you can return a minimized pop-up form to normal mode by double-clicking the caption under the icon, instead of clicking the icon itself. Users of your applications, however, likely will be unaware of this Windows quirk and will interpret the inability to maximize the form by clicking the icon as a system fault or a bug in your application.

Avoid minimizing Access's window with a pop-up form displayed

If you minimize the main (parent) Access window with a SendKeys %N action and then open a modal or modeless pop-up form, the insertion point disappears. When this situation occurs, you cannot edit text boxes in the pop-up form.

Make read-only text boxes appear and act like labels

Read-only text boxes are text boxes bound to fields of non-updatable queries and unbound text boxes with their RowSource property derived from a read-only data source. A read-only text box is equivalent to a label with an updatable Caption property; updatable labels aren't offered in Access Version 1.0.

You can speed data entry and reduce the ambiguity of controls on your form by making read-only text boxes look and act like labels. To do so, make the following changes:

1. Set the border property of read-only text boxes to Clear.

2. Apply the typeface, font size, and attributes you use for labels to the text box(es).

3. Attach a macro to the OnEnter event of each read-only text box. Add the GoToControl action with the control name of the next text box with read-write capability as the value of the Control Name property. This macro prevents the read-only text box from receiving the focus for more than a fraction of a second.

Hide text boxes attached to counter fields until you save the record

When you add new records that use a Counter field, the value of the field displays as (Counter) in a bound text box until you save the added record. Not only is this display confusing (users expect a number in this field), but you must size the text box to fit the word (Counter) rather than a few-digit number, to avoid text boxes that display ter) or the like.

To hide a text box bound to a Counter field when adding a new record, follow these steps:

1. Add a SetValue action at the end of the macro for the Add button to set the *CounterTextBox*.Visible property value to No. This SetValue action must appear after the GoToRecord action (Add) that sets the record pointer to the tentative append record.

2. Attach a macro to the OnCurrent event of the form that uses the SetValue action to set the value of the *CounterTextBox*.Visible item to Yes. You trigger the OnCurrent event when you open a form or move to a new record.

3. Add the same macro action as in step 2 to the OK button macro that saves the current record and the Cancel button macro that aborts the addition.

Speed operations by basing combo and list boxes on saved queries

Using SQL statements to populate combo and list boxes prevents your Database window's Query list from becoming cluttered. Creating and saving a query that supplies the values for combo and list boxes, however, can improve the performance of your Access application.

When you use an SQL statement as the RowSource property of a combo or list box, Access must compile the query the first time you use the combo box. When you save a QBE query, however, Access creates a compiled version. If you use the query's name as the RowSource property, Access can skip the compilation step.

Improve the performance of combo and list boxes with indexes

When filling combo or list boxes with data from a table or query with a large number of records or rows, and when the sorted or ORDER BY field isn't the primary key, add an index on the field in Table Design mode. Indexing speeds the display of records in the sort or ORDER BY sequence, at the expense of a slight degradation of performance when adding new records or saving edited records. (Access takes a measurable amount of time to update each index of a table.)

Use the Column( ) property to add values to unbound text boxes

You can use unbound combo boxes whose RowSource property is an SQL statement to assign values to unbound text boxes on a form. You can display the values in these text boxes, or set the Visible property of these text boxes to No and just use the values to emulate variables for your macros.

Populating text boxes with column values of combo boxes is a very useful technique when working with decision support forms. You need not display all the columns in the combo box to make the columns' data available to the text boxes.

Try using the Column( ) property yourself by creating sample combo boxes. Follow these steps:

1. Create a new, unbound form (leave the Select A Table/Query combo box empty) about 4 by 3 inches in size (see fig. 7.3).

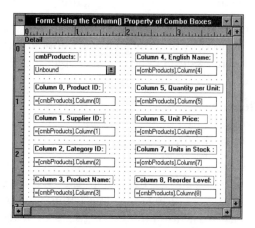

Fig. 7.3 *The use of the Column( ) property of combo boxes.*

2. Use the Toolbox to add an unbound combo box to the form. Enter **cmbProduct** as the value of the combo box's Control Name property.

3. Enter the SQL Statement **SELECT * FROM Products ORDER BY [English Name];** as the value of the RowSource property of the combo box. (Don't forget the semicolon at the end of the SQL statement.)

4. Set the value of the Column Count property to **8** and enter **0;0;0;0;1.5;0;0;0** as the value of the Column Widths property. Only the fifth column, corresponding to the English Name column of the query, appears in the combo box. Set the value of the Limit to List property to Yes.

5. Use the Toolbox to add an unbound text box to the form. Enter **=cmbProduct.Column(0)** as the value of the Control Source property for the first text box, as shown for the first text box in figure 7.3.

6. Select the label and the text box, and then press Ctrl+C to copy the control to the Clipboard. Press Ctrl+V to paste eight additional copies of the text box.

    Alternatively, you can select a group of text boxes, copy them to the Clipboard, and then paste the group to the form.

7. Edit the array element value of the Control Source property for each of the added text boxes, as shown in figure 7.3. Editing the values within the text boxes themselves is faster than changing the entries in the Properties window.

8. Change to Form Run mode and select a product name from the combo box. The values of all the columns of the selected product appear in the unbound text boxes, as shown in figure 7.4.

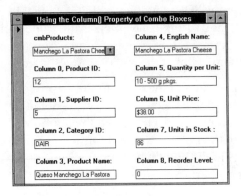

Fig. 7.4 *Displaying columns of a selection from a combo box.*

Avoid expressions containing field names in text boxes

If you try to assign an expression containing a field name, such as =[*FieldName*] + 5, and no text box on the form is bound to *FieldName*, you receive an #Error message when you switch to Form Run mode. If you need to use a field name in an expression, use an unbound text box to contain the calculated value, and then use a SetValue macro action, attached to the OnUpdate event of the text box, to set the value of a text box bound to *FieldName*. If you don't want to display the bound text box, set the value of the Visible property of the bound text box to No.

Use aliases for field names that appear more than once in a query

If you bind a text, combo, or list box to a field name that appears more than once in the query on which the form is based, you receive a #Name? error message in the box. You may have a field named Description, for example, in two tables. Consequently, Access cannot decide which Description column of the query to use, so it issues the error message.

To solve this problem, add an alias to the column you want to bind to the text box by preceding the field name with **Alias:** and then change the value of the Control Source property to *Alias*.

Use text boxes to pass criteria to queries

You can create the equivalent of a parameter query by adding an unbound text box to a form and then using the value in the text box as the criterion for a query. Add two unbound text boxes, for example, to a form into which you enter a range of dates. Name one text box Begin and the other End. Choose one date format as the value of the Format property for these text boxes. Enter

Between Forms!FormName!Begin and Forms!FormName!End

as the criterion for a field of the Time/Date data type. Add a command button to the form attached to a macro that includes an OpenQuery action to run the query with the new criterion. Enter the two dates, and then click the command button to run the query.

Note: Use the Requery macro action to update combo or list boxes based on queries with variable criteria. The Requery action reruns the query for a specified object, such as a combo or list box, to obtain the latest result. Access runs the query underlying objects on forms and reports when you open the form. After you open the form, however, Access doesn't update the query-dependent objects unless you apply the Requery action to them.

Work around fixed RowSource properties of combo and list boxes

You cannot change the RowSource property of a combo or list box programatically, but you can change the design of the query named as the value of the RowSource property. You can use an Access Basic function to alter a query in any way you choose. (See the tip "Create queries with the QueryDef( ) method" in Chapter 10, "Writing Access Basic Code that Works.") If you need to change only the criteria of a query to restrict rows returned to a selected category, for example, you can use a variable-criteria query with a choice made from a combo or list box of categories.

The following example shows how to alter a query programatically with a text box and a macro:

1. Create a new query from the Products table and add all the fields of the Products table to the query. (Don't use the * field; double-click the table's title bar, or hold the Shift key down and click each field name. Then drag the collection to the query design grid.)

2. To the form shown earlier in figure 7.4, add a combo box with a Control Name value **cmbCategory** and RowSource value **Categories**. Set the Column Count value to **2** and the Column Widths value to **0;1.5**. Set the value of Limit to List to Yes.

3. Add an ascending sort on the Product Name column and enter **Forms!FormName!cmbCategory** as the criterion of the Category ID column of the query. Save the query as *QueryName*, and then run the query and minimize its Datasheet view to an icon.

4. Delete the SQL statement from the RowSource property of the cmbProducts combo box and substitute *QueryName*. Attach *MacroName* to the OnUpdate property.

5. Create a new macro with actions shown as follows:

Action	Parameter	Value	Comment
DoMenuItem	Menu Bar Menu Name Command	Form Records Refresh	Rerun the query with the new criterion from the combo box
OpenForm	Form Name View Data Mode Window Mode	*FormName* Form Edit Normal	Set the focus to the form so that the Requery action finds the control object

continues

Action	Parameter	Value	Comment
Requery	Control Name	**cmbProducts**	Requery the combo
GoToControl	Control Name	**cmbProducts**	Set focus to combo
SendKeys	Keystrokes Wait	**{F4}{Down}** No	Open the combo box and add first entry

6. Open FormName in Form Run mode, and then open the cmbCategory combo box and choose a category. Only the products from the selected category appear in the cmbProducts combo box (see fig. 7.5).

Note: Your application needs to open the form before opening and minimizing the query when starting an application that uses the preceding technique. If you open the query before opening the form, a parameter dialog appears, because the query cannot evaluate the criterion expression that depends on the value of the form's combo box.

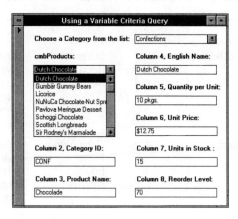

Fig. 7.5 *A form that adds query criteria from a combo box.*

Use the Format function to create special combo or list box formats

Access has no provision for applying special formatting to the data cells of combo or list boxes. If you need a special format, such as date or time, for your combo or list box column, populate the combo or list box with a query that uses the Format( ) function to create the date or time format you want. If you want a long date, for example, enter

> *AliasName*:Format([*FieldName*],"mmmm d"",
> ""yyyy")

as the value for the column in the Fields row of the query design grid.

Minimize the use of subforms to improve data-entry efficiency

Unlike main forms, subforms require inconsistent methods for entering data. Data-entry cells of subforms are below headers, and text boxes usually are located to the right of the labels that identify the text box content. To maximize data-entry efficiency, especially where a large number of entries occurs on a daily basis, avoid subforms and design individual forms for each type of data-entry operation.

Note: An exception to this suggestion applies when users are to enter columnar data, such as line items for invoices. In such cases, subform data entry is appropriate; convention invoice line-item data (quantity, item number, description, unit price, and extended amount) suits the subform model well.

Use Form view, not Datasheet view, for subforms

If you follow the design suggestions in this chapter and add record navigation command buttons to your main forms, using Datasheet view for subforms results in inconsistencies in the navigation methods between the main form and subforms. Further, you cannot control the appearance (such as background color) of subforms in Datasheet view. Thus, you should design subforms to run in Form view. Follow these steps:

1. Use the FormWizard's Main/Subform Wizard to create forms that include subforms.

2. Open the subform created by the wizard in Form Design mode and add a header and footer to the subform.

3. Move the labels for the columns to the header of the form. Select each label; then press Ctrl+X to cut the label to the Clipboard. Click the Form Header bar to select the Form Header section and press Ctrl+V to paste the label into the Form Header.

4. Relocate the text boxes under the column headers. Resize the Form Header and Detail sections of the form so that the depth of the sections equals the height of the labels and text boxes that the sections contain.

5. Set the value of the ScrollBars property to Neither.

6. Add command buttons for subform navigation to the form footer. Alternatively, set the depth of the form footer to zero and set the value of the ScrollBars property to Vertical Only.

7. Use the Palette to change the Fill color of your form sections and control objects to match the Fill color of your main form. If you have set the DefaultEditing property to ReadOnly or the AllowEditing property to Unavailable, set the Border color of the text boxes to Clear.

8. Adjust the size of the subform control on your main form to fit the design of the subform.

Figure 7.6 shows a main form/subform combination using the preceding method, based on a design in Que's *Using Access for Windows*, Special Edition. The Personnel Actions subform doesn't use vertical scroll bars because the sub-form is intended to display only the last three actions for the employee.

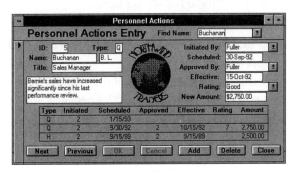

Fig. 7.6 *A subform that matches the overall design of the main form.*

Disable command buttons that don't apply to the current state of your form

Set the value of the Enabled property of command buttons to No when the actions they trigger don't apply to the current status of your form. This way, you can prevent users of your applications from attempting an invalid action.

The OK and Cancel buttons of the form shown in figure 7.6, for example, are disabled until the user edits or adds a record. While the user is editing or adding records, the OK and Cancel buttons are enabled and the remaining buttons are disabled. After the user chooses OK or Cancel to accept or reject the changes or additions to the records, those buttons return to their disabled status and the remaining buttons are enabled.

Although attaching a macro that sets the Enabled properties of several buttons to the OnUpdate event of each text box in your form requires a good deal of typing, it provides substantial benefits to the form's users.

Use special syntax to obtain the value of a cell on a subform

To obtain the value of a data cell of the selected row of a subform, you must use the following special syntax that isn't referenced in the Microsoft Access *User's Guide* (although this syntax is buried in the *Language Reference* under the heading "Form, Report Properties"):

Forms!MainFormName!SubformName.Form!ColumnName

Note the distinction between the plural **Forms**, the identifier for an object class, and the singular **Form**, a property of a control. This syntax is the *only* method by which you can obtain the value of a cell of a subform. The value is returned from the cell of the currently selected record of the subform. Use the same syntax for subreports, but change **Forms!** to **Reports!** and **Form!** to **Report!**

Note: You can use the Form property to identify the current form in a macro, as in **Form!***ControlName*. When you use **Forms!**, you must add the name of the form after the bang symbol (!). Using **Form!** to identify the current form in macros isn't recommended, because it doesn't indicate the name of the form when you print the macro details for documentation purposes. Use the full syntax, **Forms!***FormName***!***ControlName*, to avoid ambiguity.

Attach a macro to the double-click event of subform text boxes

If you have insufficient display area to include command buttons in the Footer section of your subform, you can open a form used to edit the subform data. Do so by attaching a macro to the double-click event of one or more bound text boxes that display subform data. Add an OpenForm action to the macro that opens the editing form as a dialog.

You also can use the double-click event of a subform text box to open a dialog containing a list box of values appropriate for the field, prompting the user for valid entries.

Set the focus to the subform before you use the GoToRecord macro action

Using a GoToRecord action in a macro attached to a main form that specifies the subform as the Object Name results in the erroneous error message `Object 'SubformName' isn't open`. If this message were true, the subform wouldn't appear on your form. You need to add a GoToControl action that specifies the name of the subform (to set the focus to the subform control) before you use the GoToRecord action to set the position of the subform's record pointer.

CHAPTER

Designing and Printing Professional Reports

Access provides a versatile report generator that rivals or exceeds the report generation capability of any other Windows RDBMS. This chapter provides tips on creating standard templates, overcoming report printing problems, and designing reports that deliver the information you need in a visually attractive style.

Create a custom template for standard reports

Access's default dimensions for new reports are 5 inches wide and 1 1/2 inches deep (a 1-inch-deep Detail section with 1/4-inch Page Header and Page Footer). The default template omits the Report Header and Report Footer sections.

If you use a standard 8 1/2-by-11-inch format for your reports, set the width of the report to 8.5 inches, less the combined width of your standard margins. Add standard objects, such as your firm's logo, to the Report Header, and standard date and page number controls to the Page Footer section. Save the custom report template in your current database; then copy the template to the Clipboard and paste the copy, giving the copy the name of your report. (Better yet, follow the next tip and create a new database that you use only to store templates.) Import the template from the template database when you begin a new report or form design.

Create a template database for reports and forms

If you want to use standard templates for reports that incorporate logo and other standard control objects, create a new template database to store the standard reports. Don't bother substituting the name of your custom template for the Normal (default) template in the Form & Report Design category of the Options dialog. Although Access stores the name of the custom template in SYSTEM.MDA, the template must exist in each database that uses the named template. If the custom template isn't present in the database, you get the standard 5-inch wide Normal template. When you create a new form or report, Access omits any graphic or control objects that appear on your custom template.

Use the Printing options to set default margins

Access's default printing margins are a conservative 1 inch for the top, bottom, and sides of reports. Most laser printers have an 8-by-10 1/2-inch or more printable area on letter-size paper. Narrower margins enable you to place more data on a page or use a font larger than Access's default 8-point size. You can change the values of the default printing margins for reports by choosing View Options and then selecting the Printing category.

Specify unique print setup information for individual reports

Access saves print setup information with each form or report. When you change the default values in the Print Setup dialog, Access saves the changes with the current report when you close the Print Setup dialog. As a result, you can assign special printer setup information—such as different printers, margins, and number of items across—to specific reports.

This Access capability isn't available in many other mainstream Windows applications in which the setup information you select applies to all the documents you print.

Note: When you set new default margins, the change applies only to reports you create from that point onward. Previously created reports maintain the original default values, because Access stored those values with the reports. You must go back and change the margin settings of each of these reports to the new default setting if you want the top and left margin of all your reports to be identical. (The design of your report rather than margin settings may determine the bottom and right margins.)

Have your margins correspond to the printable area of your laser printer

If you set a form's margins to a value less than the dimensions of the border defining the printable area of your laser printer, your printed reports may look distorted or omit characters that fall outside the printed area. Access doesn't test the margins you set (as default values or in the Print Setup dialog) against the printable area of your printer. Access doesn't test the margins because printers used by others who share or use your reports may have different printable area limitations. Be sure to set the

margins within the printable area of *all* the printers used
by your workgroup or by those that share your database
applications.

Specify the Default Printer if you plan to share your database on a network

 If workgroup members who share your database have different types of local printers, be
sure to specify the Default Printer, not a Specific
Printer, in the Print Setup dialog. This setting is especially
important if some users have PostScript printers and others have Hewlett-Packard laser printers or printers using
the HP PCL (Printer Control Language) protocol. A
PostScript printer, for example, may substitute the Zapf
Dingbats typeface for Windows System fonts, leading to
misprinted reports.

When you select the Default Printer, the system uses the
printer driver that each user has chosen for his or her local
default printer, and each user may choose the proper font
substitution and other options for his or her local printer.

Note: When you specify the Default Printer, you and all
who share your database must select a default printer
using the Printers function of Windows Control Panel. If
you specify Default Printer but fail to choose a default
printer for your system, you receive an error message
when you try to create a new report.

Use TrueType fonts to accommodate the widest range of printers

If you need to use various types of printers for your reports, use TrueType fonts, because they accommodate the
widest range of printers. TrueType fonts, introduced with
Windows 3.1, also are similar or identical in appearance to
the typeface families you choose for your reports.

Access uses the Arial typeface in an 8-point font as the default for printing reports. Arial's 8-point font looks similar to the MS Sans Serif font, the default for Form and Datasheet views. You can change the default font by providing a default Font Name and size property for reports in the Form & Report Design category.

Use Print Setup to change the default Arial typeface

If you prefer Linotype's Helvetica or its clones (usually called Swiss on PCL printers) rather than the more stylized Arial type family, and you have a PostScript or laser printer driver that offers type substitution options, you can map Arial to the desired face. Follow these steps:

1. Choose File Print Setup and click the Options button of the Print Setup dialog.

2. Click the Advanced button of the Options dialog, if it appears.

   Note: If the Advanced button doesn't appear, your laser printer driver doesn't offer typeface substitution, and you can skip the rest of this tip.

3. Click the Edit Substitution Table button of the Advanced Options dialog.

4. Select Arial in the For TrueType Font list box; then click the typeface you want to substitute for Arial in the Use Printer Font list box.

If your printer driver offers typeface substitution, Access saves the typeface substitution data in your WIN.INI file, not with the report or in the SYSTEM.MDA file. Your typeface substitutions don't affect those of other workgroup members. When you use a PostScript printer, the [PSCRIPT] section of WIN.INI contains entries such as

`Arial=Helvetica`. Consequently, the typeface substitutions you make apply to all reports in all databases, as well as any other Windows applications that use the TrueType faces you mapped.

Print TrueType fonts as graphics with the HP LaserJet II family

The Windows printer driver for the HP LaserJet II family of printers doesn't support the use of outline fonts, such as TrueType and Adobe Type 1. To use TrueType fonts with most HP LaserJet II printers, you must send the characters to be printed as bit maps (graphic images) to the printer. Choose File Print Setup; then click the Options button. In the Options dialog, mark the Print TrueType as Graphics check box in the lower left corner.

Use the Print TrueType Graphics option to print reverse type

If you use reverse TrueType (white or light gray type on a black or dark gray background) in your reports and use an HP LaserJet printer with the standard PCL driver, only the dark background may appear when you print the report. If you need reverse type (most commonly used in page headers), set the Print TrueType as Graphics option by the method described in the preceding tip.

Note: If you use the PostScript driver with a PostScript-equipped LaserJet printer, reverse type prints correctly. No changes are required, whether you map the TrueType faces or download TrueType fonts as PostScript (Adobe Type 1) soft fonts.

Save forms as reports for printing

You can save the orms you design as reports and then modify the resulting report as necessary for proper printing. Open the form in Design mode; then choose File Save As Report. Enter the name you want for the report in the Save Form as Report dialog.

Note: Continuous forms are the best candidates for conversion to reports.

Eliminate large shaded areas on forms you save as reports

Extensive areas of shading—even light gray—detract from the appearance of your report. Large shaded areas also require substantial amounts of expensive toner.

Forms often use a gray background, and some forms (including many of those of the Northwind Traders sample database) use quite dark backgrounds. If you save a form as a report, change the background color to Clear or white, and then change the fill color of text boxes and other control objects to match the background.

Change the Selection Behavior option to suit your design preference

In most drawing applications, you select objects by enclosing them within a rectangle. You drag the rectangle to completely enclose all the objects you want to select; partially enclosed graphic objects remain unselected. Access, however, by default selects all control objects that the selection rectangle encloses or touches.

If you are accustomed to using Microsoft Draw, Micrografx Windows Draw, or CorelDRAW!, you can change the Access selection behavior setting to match the selection behavior of those applications. This change can help you avoid accidentally selecting a control object by touching it with the Access selection rectangle.

To change Access's selection behavior setting, choose View Options, select the Form & Report Design category, and then change the value of the Selection Behavior property from Partially Enclosed to Fully Enclosed.

Note: In general, designers space control objects more closely together on reports than on forms.

Use the OutputAs library to print reports to a file

You can insert an Access report into another document and then print the combined document by saving the report to a file with the OutputAs library (OUTPUTAS.MDA) and DLL (OUTPUTAS.DLL), and then importing the file into your document.

To obtain the OutputAs library, download OUTPUT.ZIP from the Reports/Printing library of the MSACCESS forum on CompuServe. Instructions for using the OutputAs library are included in README.TXT and OUTPUTAS.TXT, included in OUTPUT.ZIP. Tips on using third-party libraries and wizards, a special type of library, are included in Chapter 12, "Taking Advantage of Libraries and Wizards."

Design reports specifically for saving as files with OutputAs

OutputAs has several limitations that affect the printed appearance of reports you save to a file. OutputAs doesn't reproduce graphic objects in files or include data from sub-reports. OutputAs can export files in RTF (Rich Text Format, used by Word for Windows and other Windows word processing applications), XLS (BIFF, the Excel data interchange format), and TXT (ANSI text file format).

Each output format has its own set of capabilities and oddities. You must design your report to suit the output format you choose. The rule is, the simpler the report format, the better the appearance of the destination document.

Note: OutputAs inserts spurious newline pairs (paragraphs without content) and formats paragraphs with one line after in RTF files. After you import the report file, you must clean up the text considerably in Word for Windows. Notice that the text in the Page Header is truncated. You must expand the width of text boxes substantially to ensure that their entire content appears when you use RTF format.

Use BIFF format with OutputAs for best results in most cases

Use OutputAs's BIFF format, which creates an Excel XLS worksheet file, to minimize post-import reformatting. BIFF preserves the formatting you apply to text boxes and doesn't truncate the content of text boxes. You can import the resulting worksheet, with little or no formatting in Excel, to a table in Word for Windows. This process eliminates the extensive reformatting required when you import RTF files to Word for Windows.

Note: BIFF format places the vertically stacked argument fields that appear in the report (and in the RTF file) in individual columns of Excel worksheets. The resulting worksheet is very wide and difficult to handle. BIFF format is best used for detail sections that consist of a single row of text boxes (the most common design for forms).

Adjust margins to avoid printing problems with some mailing labels

The ReportWizard makes the assumption that for 8 1/2-by-11-inch sheets, your printer has a printable area at least 8 inches wide and, in some cases (such as Avery 4144 labels), as much as 10 3/4 inches long. If your printer cannot handle a 10 3/4-inch printing length, it may print only the bottoms of the characters in the first line of your label, or omit the first line completely.

To correct this situation, you can skip the first label by adding the depth of the label to the top margin set by the ReportWizard. In the case of Avery 4144 labels, the original top margin is 0.03 inch and the depth of the labels is 15/16 (0.9375) inch; as a result, change the top margin to 0.97 inch. Access then reduces the number of rows of labels from 11 to 10.

Note: If your laser printer becomes misaligned and the image area (called the *logical page*) has shifted with respect to the edges of the paper (called the *physical page*), you may need to adjust the margins of your mailing labels in the Print Setup dialog to compensate for the misalignment.

If the last row of labels doesn't print correctly, increase the bottom margin by the depth of one label. If your laser printer and Windows printer driver support legal-size (8 1/2-by-14-inch) paper, you probably can print all the labels on an 11-inch-deep sheet if you adjust the bottom margin; if not, you lose the last row of labels on the sheet.

Note: Avery labels 4143, 4160, and 5096 are designed specifically for use with dot-matrix printers. Don't select these stock numbers if you are using a laser printer.

Change the ReportWizard's font size for mailing labels

The default font for mailing labels created by the Mailing Label Wizard is 8-point Arial. The U.S. Postal Service, however, prefers a larger font for mailing addresses. Most mailing labels are designed for 12-point fonts (6 lines per inch). Using 12-point Courier New, which the new postal scanners handle well, may speed the delivery of your mailings.

To change the ReportWizard's font for mailing labels, follow these steps:

1. Open your mailing label report in Design view, select all the text boxes, and change the typeface and font with the toolbar's combo boxes.

2. Because you need the additional space occupied by the margins within the labels, move the grouped text boxes to the left margin of the report design window. Then extend the width of the text boxes to the right margin.

3. Set the value of the Can Grow property of each text box to No, to truncate lines longer than the width of your label.

4. Switch to Print Preview mode to verify that the ZIP codes aren't missing because of long city names. If this problem occurs, change to an 11-point font.

Note: Setting the value of the dimensions of the text box in the Properties window can be easier than adjusting the width and depth of each text box with the mouse. Suppose that the top margin of the first line of your labels is 0.05 inch, and that each text box is 0.2 inch high. In this example, the value of the Top property settings of the subsequent text boxes are 0.25, 0.45, 0.65, and so on. If your printer doesn't print the first line of the top label properly, set the Top of the first line of the label to 0.15 inch and the Height property of each text box to 0.18 inch, adjusting the Top values of the remaining text boxes in 0.18-inch increments.

Use separate fields, not new-line characters, for compound addresses

Some of your tables may include Address fields with embedded newline characters created by pressing Ctrl+Enter, used to produce two-line addresses (to separate suite numbers from street addresses, for example, or to distinguish elements of compound addresses). Tables that include two-line fields create problems when you try to print them in mailing labels.

Using two-line fields violates the rule of first normal form for relational databases: Each field (column) of a table must contain *only one* type of data entity. Secondary address entities are different from street address entities; street addresses are mandatory, secondary addresses are optional. Thus, you should add a field, such as Address2, to contain optional secondary addresses.

Note: Two-line fields also cause problems when you use 15/16-inch deep mailing labels (the most common variety) with 12-point type. If you set the value of the Can Grow property to Yes, you lose the City, State, Zip Code line of the label. If you set the value of the Can Grow property to No, you lose the second line of the field value for the label.

Avoid using SQL statements as data sources for reports

You can use a valid SQL SELECT statement as the Record Source for a form, but not for a report. If you try to base a report on an SQL SELECT statement, you receive an error message, followed by your SQL statement.

9

CHAPTER

Working with Pictures and Graphs

This chapter supplies tips for displaying the images you store in tables or add to forms and reports. Microsoft Graph, supplied with Access, and the GraphWizard work together to generate graphs and charts from your data. This chapter includes tips for creating professional-appearing Access graphs and charts that put your data in perspective.

Note: Knowing the differences in the use and behavior of bound and unbound object frames aids in understanding the following tips. If you need a clearer understanding of bound and unbound object frames, read Que's *Using Access for Windows*, Special Edition.

Add auto-update capability to objects in bound object frames

You manually can update an object in a bound object frame by selecting the object frame, choosing *ObjectType* Object from the Edit menu, and choosing Update Now from the submenu. You can emulate auto-update by attaching a macro with a DoMenuItem action to the OnCurrent event of your form.

If your OLE Object field contains linked and embedded objects, you need to add a Yes/No field, Is Linked, to indicate whether the object is linked or embedded. Then add the condition [**Is Linked**] to the DoMenuItem action to prevent a Command unavailable message when you try to update an embedded object.

Track the source of images in OLE object fields with an added field

When your tables include a substantial number of images, losing track of their original source files is easy. Add a field to tables that contain embedded or linked images to identify the file name and location of the image. If the image is located on removable media, such as a CD-ROM or Photo CD, you need another field to identify the volume that includes the original file.

Enable users to edit OLE objects with a common OLE server application

 You don't need access to the OLE server that you used to embed or link the OLE object to your table to display an image, because its presentation is stored in the OLE field of your table. If you want users of your application to be able to edit the image, they need access to the same OLE server you used to link or embed the image. If other users don't have the required OLE server, they receive a Server Not Available message when they double-click the linked or embedded image, or try to update a linked image.

Displaying linked, full-size images represented by thumb-nail presentations with an OLE server such as Lenel Systems' MultiMedia Works also requires user access to the OLE server. (This topic is the subject of tips in Chapter 3, "Designing and Using Access Tables.") Users need Media Player 3.1 or its equivalent to play waveform audio and MIDI objects. If you embed or link only waveform audio data, Windows 3.1's Sound Recorder is adequate.

Prevent editing of bound OLE objects by setting the Enabled property to No

Unless the users of your application have graphic arts skills, you probably don't want them to be able to edit the images contained in OLE Object fields of your tables. Set the value of the Enabled property to No to prevent all users of your application from launching the OLE server that created the image. Alternatively, you can convert the image to a picture, breaking the link to the originating server, to prevent editing.

Intercept the double-click event to select objects the user can edit

If you want to give the user the capability to edit specific images, or if you use an OLE server, attach a macro to the double-click event. Use the CancelEvent action to prevent the double-click event from launching the server.

To control editing capability, you can add a condition, based on the value of a Yes/No field or the presence of specific logon names of users. In a secure system, where a logon name and PIN (personal identification number) identifies each user, the User() function returns the logon name of the current user of your application. The default user name that Access assigns is Admin. Chapter 11, "Networking Access," provide tips on using Access's built-in security system.

Add graphics to OLE Object fields in bound object frames

Chapter 3, "Designing and Using Access Tables," includes tips on how to add embedded and linked OLE objects to your tables in Datasheet view. You can use the same methods to add new images to records you append to tables with a form. Select the bound object frame with a single click (or press Tab to move to the bound object frame). Access adds a pixel-wide dotted border inside the object's frame to identify a selected object frame (with the focus). Then choose Edit Insert Object to embed an OLE object in the frame.

To link a file, open the OLE server application independently of Access, load the file you want to link, select the image, and copy the selected image to the Clipboard. Then choose Edit Paste Link or Edit Paste Special to link the file to the bound object frame.

Use a macro to automate addition of embedded OLE objects

If you are adding many images to a table, you can streamline the process by attaching a macro to perform the menu operations required to embed an OLE object. Add the DoMenuItem action to the macro with File as the Menu Bar argument and Insert Object as the Menu Item. Use the SendKeys action to enter {Down} keystrokes in the Object Type list box to select the OLE server, followed by %F to open the Insert Object from File dialog. Then choose the file whose data you want to embed. (This tip applies only to embedded objects, *not* to linked objects.)

Note: If you add another OLE server or remove an OLE server from your computer, the number of {Down} keystrokes required to select the desired object type may change. Don't use the preceding technique for applications to be used by others, because their list of OLE servers may be different from yours.

Create a single graph derived from multiple rows of a query or table

The most popular style of graph in the business environment is the time-series line graph that displays values (usually monetary) in the vertical axis (Y-axis or abscissa) and time in the horizontal axis (X-axis or ordinate). As a result, most graphs you create are likely based on crosstab queries with time periods (such as months, quarters, or years) in column headings, and the summary data you want to compare in rows of the query. Create a new form with the GraphWizard, if you want one graph that includes a line representing the values in each row of the crosstab query. See the next tip if you want to create a graph that displays only the line for one row of your crosstab query.

When you use the GraphWizard to create a form, the resulting line graph is linked to the entire query, not to individual records of the query. The graph, therefore, includes a line for each row in the query. Figure 9.1 shows a graph, as created by the new form GraphWizard, that is based on a crosstab query that calculates total sales by category of Northwind's products for the year 1991. The query for this graph is described in Chapter 8 of *Using Access for Windows*, Special Edition, published by Que Corporation.

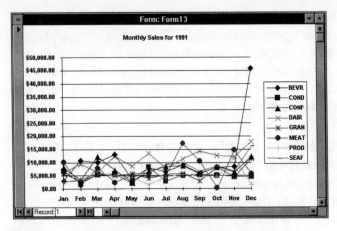

Fig. 9.1 *The multiple-value graph that results from creating a new form with the GraphWizard.*

Limit the number of categories you display with a single-line graph

Figure 9.1 displays sales by month for eight product categories—about four too many sets of time-series values to display on a single graph. As a rule of thumb, four lines on a single graph is the maximum for readability.

Create individual queries that return a maximum of four rows; then use the GraphWizard to generate a separate graph based on each query. Use a criterion to limit the number of rows. Add **In (BEVR, COND, CONF, DAIR)** to the Criteria row of the Category ID field of the Monthly Sales for 1991 query, for example, to limit the number of lines to four. (Access adds the quotation marks around the arguments of the In operator for you.)

Display widely varying values clearly with logarithmic Y-axis scaling

The extraordinary sales performance shown in figure 9.1 for the BEVR category in December 1991 results in a maximum value of the Y-axis of the chart of $50,000. This dramatic increase causes the data for other categories and months to be "buried" at the bottom of the graph. To create a more readable (and thus meaningful) graph, change the Y-axis scaling from Linear to Logarithmic mode by following these steps:

1. Open the form that contains the graph in Design mode; then double-click the graph to launch the Microsoft Graph OLE server.

2. Click a value in the Y-axis scale to select the Y-axis (indicated by small squares at the top and bottom of the Y-axis line).

3. Choose Scale from Graph's Format menu. The Format Axis Scale dialog appears.

4. Mark the Logarithmic Scale check box, change the Minimum value for the Y-axis to 1000, and then choose OK to close the dialog.

   Note: If you leave the Minimum value at its default value of 1, your data will be buried in the middle of the graph.

5. Choose File Exit to Microsoft Access to return to Access Design mode.

6. Click the Run Mode toolbar button to display the changes to your graph. The Monthly Sales for 1991 graph with a logarithmically scaled Y-axis is shown in figure 9.2.

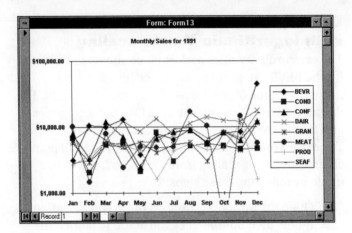

Fig. 9.2 *The graph of figure 9.1 with the Y-axis changed from linear to logarithmic scaling.*

Note: Sales for the MEAT category dropped precipitously in October (to $288). Because the value is less than the Minimum Y-axis scale value, the sales value symbol for October doesn't appear on the graph.

Use area or bar charts to display contribution of row values to totals

If you want to show the total of the Y-axis values, convert your line graph to an area chart. Contribution of individual values to the total is displayed by differently colored areas. Figure 9.3 shows the graph of figure 9.1 converted to an area chart.

Use patterns rather than colors when printing area charts in reports

Printing the area chart of figure 9.3 results in large areas of dark colors on the report. Some laser printers don't print large dark areas evenly and often have problems with printing reverse (white) type in these areas. Large dark areas also consume extraordinary amounts of toner.

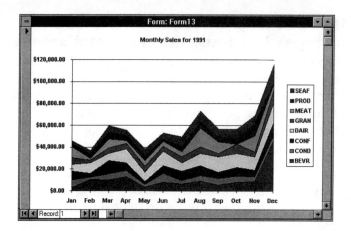

Fig. 9.3 *An area chart showing monthly sales totals and the contribution of individual values to the total.*

You can convert the colored areas of area charts on forms to half-tone screens—that is, patterns—whose density you can control for printing reports. Figure 9.4 shows an area graph converted to half-tone screens.

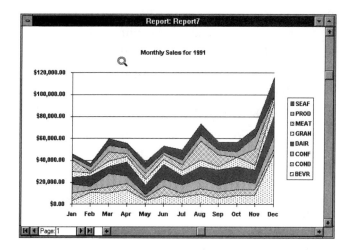

Fig. 9.4 *A graph from a form modified for printing in a report.*

Use 100% column charts to display changes in composition of total values

Only a few of GraphWizard's numerous types of graphs and charts are shown on its opening form. One type of chart often requested by management displays individual sets of values as a percent of the totals of the values. Pie charts (discussed later) display the percentage composition of a total value.

You can use a 100% column chart to display multiple compositions, such as distribution of sales by product category, in a time series. Because 100% column charts aren't included in the GraphWizard's repertoire, you need to create one of the Wizard's offerings, and then change the chart type in Microsoft Chart. Follow these steps to create a 100% column chart:

1. Open a new form and use the GraphWizard to create a multiple-value line chart. Alternatively, if you want to convert an existing line chart, double-click the chart in Design mode to launch MS Graph.

2. Choose Chart from Graph's Format menu to display the Format Chart dialog. (You don't need to select the chart for the Chart menu item to appear.)

3. Choose Column from the Chart Type combo box; then click the button with the chart that has two equal-height bars, symbolizing a 100% column chart.

4. Choose OK. Your line chart is converted to a 100% column chart, with appropriate changes to the X-axis scale.

5. Choose File Exit and Return to Microsoft Access. In the message box that appears, choose Yes to update your chart.

Figure 9.5 shows a 100% column chart created from the line chart shown in figure 9.1.

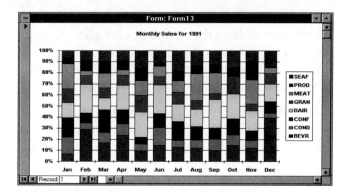

Fig. 9.5 *A GraphWizard line chart converted to a 100% column chart.*

Create a graph linked to individual records of a form's data source

You need to use the Toolbox's graph tool in Form or Report Design mode to create a single-line graph that is linked to the data in the current record of the form. You can establish a link between the data displayed by the graph and the form in the same way that you establish a link between main form and subform data: set the values of the Link Child Fields and Link Master Fields properties to one or more fields in the table or query.

To create a graph that displays values from each row of the underlying query or table as you change the record pointer, follow these steps:

1. Open a new blank form based on the query or table that supplies the data to the form and the graph.

2. Click the graph tool and drag until the rectangle is the desired size of the graph. When you release the mouse button, the GraphWizard's form appears.

3. Select the name of the table or query on which your form is based from the combo box list, click the line chart, click the Add Legend check box to remove the default X (if the check box appears), and then click the Next button.

4. Select the fields of your query or table to be included in the graph, and then click the Next button. You must include in this list the field that you use to link the graph and the form.

5. Select the fields to be used as labels for your graph, if GraphWizard requests you to do so. Don't include the field that you use to link the graph to the form in this list. Click the Next button. In the message box that appears, choose Yes to link the graph to the form.

6. Choose the fields you use to link the graph to the form from the Form fields and Graph fields list boxes, and then click the <=> button to create the link. The underlying data source of the graph and form is the same, so the linking field names are identical. The link you created appears in the Link(s) list box. Click the Next button.

7. Click the Design button to return to Form Design mode; then click the Run toolbar button to display your linked graph. Click the Next Record selector button to show that the graph is indeed linked to the current record of your form.

Figure 9.6 shows the graph as created by the GraphWizard for the Monthly Sales for 1991 query, used in the examples of the previous tips.

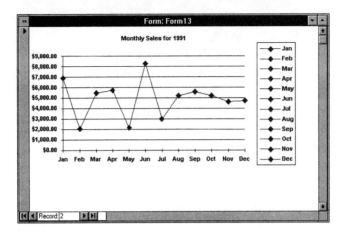

Fig. 9.6 *A graph linked to a form created by the Toolbox's graph tool.*

Note: The combo box in which you selected the data source for your graph doesn't appear when you use the GraphWizard to create a new form, nor does the dialog that asks whether you want to link your graph to the form. These two steps enable you to link the graph to the current record of the form and distinguish the Toolbox's GraphWizard from the GraphWizard that you use to create a new form.

Change to Run mode to add data to a blank graph

When you create a graph that is linked to the current record of a form or report, the graph appears as a blank object frame until you change to Run mode (or Print Preview mode, in the case of reports). The graph needs the data from the current record to create an initial presentation, which is available only after you run the graph once.

Graphs in new forms created by the GraphWizard also appear blank if you click the Design button rather than the Preview button. If you double-click the blank graph, the graph in MS Graph is equally featureless. Always click the Preview button to display your graph as the last step in the new form from GraphWizard process.

Use fixed maximum Y-axis values to ensure consistency among graphs

Graphs linked to successive records that underlie the form usually are used for comparison purposes. By default, Microsoft Graph establishes the maximum Y-axis value of the graph from the data for each instance of the graph. (When you change the current record, a new graph, called an *instance*, is created from the data in the current record.) You can ensure consistency between graphs by following these steps to establish a fixed maximum value:

1. Double-click the graph in Design mode to launch MS Graph.

2. Select the Y-axis in Graph and choose Format Scale.

3. Enter a reasonable maximum value that applies to all instances of the graph in the Maximum text box of the Format Axis Scale dialog; then choose OK.

4. Choose File Exit from Microsoft Access to return to Access; then click the Run Mode toolbar button to test the result.

Eliminate the need to switch between modes when editing graphs

When you make changes to graphs with the Microsoft Graph OLE server, you can save time by temporarily setting to Yes the value of the Enabled property of the unbound object frame that contains your graph. This way, you eliminate the need to switch between Design and Run modes, and the wait while the OLE server loads the new instance of the graph. Changes you make in Microsoft Graph are reflected in the current instance of the graph when you exit MS Graph and return to Access.

Show distribution of totals with 3-D pie charts

You can display individual three-dimensional pie charts that show composition of a total value, such as sales distribution by product, on a periodic basis (by month, for example). Create a crosstab query that uses the column values (months) of the conventional crosstab query used for the preceding examples to generate row values, and the row values (categories) to provide column headings in the new query. In effect, you rotate the Datasheet view of the query 90 degrees counter-clockwise. Figure 9.7 shows the design of the query required to place categories in column headers and months in rows.

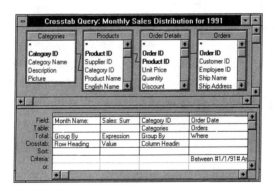

Fig. 9.7 *The Monthly Sales query revised for categories in columns and months in rows.*

Enter **Month Name:Format([Orders].[Order Date],"mmmm")** to create the row headings. This expression is identical to the expression used for column headings in the query of the previous examples, except for the long month name format (*mmmm* replaces *mmm*). Values of Category ID, previously used for the row headings, now become the column headings. The entry for the Sales field is as follows:

> **Sales: Sum([Order Details].[Quantity]*[Order Details].[Unit Price])**

The complete syntax for the Criteria of the Order Date field is

> **Between #1/1/91# And #12/31/91#**

In addition to creating the query, make a Months of the Year table to act as the data source for your form so that you can link the name of the month of the current record with that of the query. Each record in this table has the month number (1 to 12, an integer), the primary key, and the full name of the month (January to December).

Rather than use the table, you can add another column to the query—the month number with an ascending sort—but this procedure links the graph to another data source. If you don't add the ascending sort on the month number, your first record is for April, the second is for December, and so on.

Save your table and query; then follow these steps to create a month-by-month pie chart for sales distribution by category:

1. Create a new, blank form based on the Months of the Year table.

2. Using the graph tool, add an unbound object to display the graph. Choose the new query, Monthly Sales

Distribution for 1991, as the data source for the graph, click the three-dimensional pie chart button, and then click the Next button.

3. Add all the fields of the query as fields to include in your graph, and click the Next button.

4. Add only the eight category fields (not Month Name) for the labels of the graph, make sure that the Add Legend check box is marked, and click the Next button.

5. In the message box that appears, choose Yes to link the table to the graph. Select the Month Name fields from the query and the table to create the link. Click the <=> button and then click the Next button.

6. Click the Design button to create the graph. After the wizard is finished, set the value of the Enabled property of the graph's object frame to Yes; then click the Run Mode toolbar button to display the graph.

   The labels for the pie wedges display the Category ID values, not the percentages of total sales for the month.

7. Double-click the graph to launch MS Graph. Choose Chart Data Labels, click the Show Percent button, and then choose OK.

8. Choose File Exit and Return to Microsoft Access to display your revised pie chart, similar to that shown in figure 9.8.

Use Text fields to link graphs to forms with GraphWizard Version 1.0

You shouldn't try to link a graph based on a query to a form based on a different query or table with fields having a number data type such as Integer. If you try this link,

Version 1.0 of the GraphWizard displays an `Illegal function call` message box about halfway through the process of creating the graph. This problem occurs with the GraphWizard, not with MS Graph.

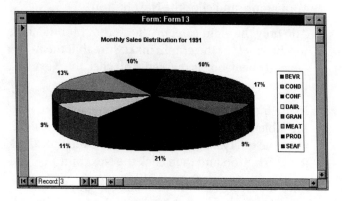

Fig. 9.8 *The sales distribution pie chart for March 1991.*

Use a field of the Text, rather than the Number, data type to link the graph to the form. You can verify whether your version of the GraphWizard has this problem by changing the field entry for Month Name of the query to **Month: Month([Orders].[Order Date])** and trying to create a link between the Month field of the query and the Month field of the Months of the Year table that underlies the form.

Note: You can modify the link to use two number fields as the values of the Link Child Fields and Link Master Fields properties of your unbound object box after you success-fully create the graph with the GraphWizard using Text field links. Make sure that you change the name of the fields (`[Month Name]` to `[Month]`, for example) in the SQL statement that serves as the value of the Row Source property of the graph's object frame.

Speed up display by replacing linked graphs with a static version

Management and supervisory personnel, for whom you are likely to create most of your forms and reports that contain graphs, aren't noted for their patience. Unless your users have a very fast computer and a fast hard drive, graphs in bound or unbound object boxes take a considerable time to display. You can make users of your Access applications that contain graphs happier with the performance of your product by converting graphs based on data that doesn't change to static drawing objects.

If your firm's auditors have completed their annual report for the last fiscal year, for example, sales data for that year shouldn't change. All graphs based on sales data for the prior and earlier fiscal years, therefore, are candidates for freezing.

Follow these steps to convert dynamic graphs to static graphs on a production-line basis, using the pie chart in figure 9.8 as an example:

1. Open the Months of Year table (see the preceding tip for its basic structure and content) in Design view and add an OLE Object field named Graphs.

2. Open your form that contains the unbound object frame with monthly graphs in Design mode. Decrease the size of the object frame, if necessary, so that another object frame can fit on the form. Set the value of the Enabled property to Yes.

3. Open the Field List window and drag the Graphs field to the form. Size the resulting bound object frame as desired. (The frame doesn't need to display the entire graph now.)

4. Change to Form Run mode and select the first record of the table. Double-click the bound object frame containing the graph to launch Microsoft Graph.

5. Press Ctrl+C or choose Edit Copy Chart to copy the chart to the Clipboard; then choose File Exit to return to Access.

6. Select the empty bound object frame and choose File Insert Object. Select Microsoft Drawing from the Object Type list box and click OK.

7. When Microsoft Draw's window appears, press Ctrl+V or choose Edit Paste.

   Note: You may want to change the typeface and size, because not all typefaces and fonts reproduce identically in MS Graph and Draw.

8. Choose File Exit and Return to Microsoft Access to update your bound object box with the drawing of the graph.

9. Repeat steps 5 through 8 for each record of the form.

You can automate the process further by attaching a macro to the OnCurrent event of the form (with the condition **IsNull([Graphs])**) that performs the sequence of keystrokes and menu choices described in steps 5 through 8.

Note: You can speed exiting OLE servers by double-clicking the application control box at the upper left corner of the servers' window to return to Access.

Hide the title of a graph by changing its color

No matter how hard you try, you cannot eliminate the title at the top of the chart. If you leave the title of the graph blank in the last form of the GraphWizard, Access substitutes the title *Graph*. You can make the title blend into the chart's background, however, by changing the color of the title to the background color. Launch MS Graph and click the title to select it. Choose Format Font and choose the background color from the Color combo box. Click the Transparent option button in the Background frame. Your title disappears.

Note: Although the title of the graph is transparent, you cannot adjust the position of the graph relative to the top of MS Graph's window to reduce the top margin in your unbound object frame.

10

Writing Access Basic Code that Works

You likely can design 95 percent of the applications you write without using any Access Basic code. The built-in macro actions of Access are surprisingly versatile. You may find after you learn the ins and outs of Access Basic, however, that you prefer writing code to picking macro actions, especially for complex event handlers. The choice is up to you.

This chapter gives you tips on extending the capabilities of Access with Access Basic code. The tips range in scope from beginning- to advanced-level code.

In examples of Access Basic code throughout this book, monospace type is used to distinguish Access Basic code from descriptive text (except in headings). Access Basic keywords and intrinsic constants are in **boldfaced monospace** type; all constants are in uppercase letters, the convention for symbolic constants declared in the C language. Variable names and other names that require substitution of a name appropriate to your application are in *monospace italic*.

Note: Access Basic shares many common characteristics with Visual Basic 2.0, but if you're a Visual Basic programmer, you should be aware of two fundamental differences: Access doesn't assign names automatically to event-handling code, and functions, not sub-procedures, are used to respond to events.

Use the Immediate Window to experiment with Access Basic

You can use the Immediate Window to gain a better understanding of the **Variant** data type, by experimenting with variables of different data types and the built-in functions of Access Basic. Open the Introduction to Programming module and then choose View Immediate Window. Assign values to *ad hoc* variables in the Immediate Window and then test the variables with Access functions. (You cannot use the **Dim** statement in the Immediate Window.) Figure 10.1 shows the Immediate Window with some of the expressions.

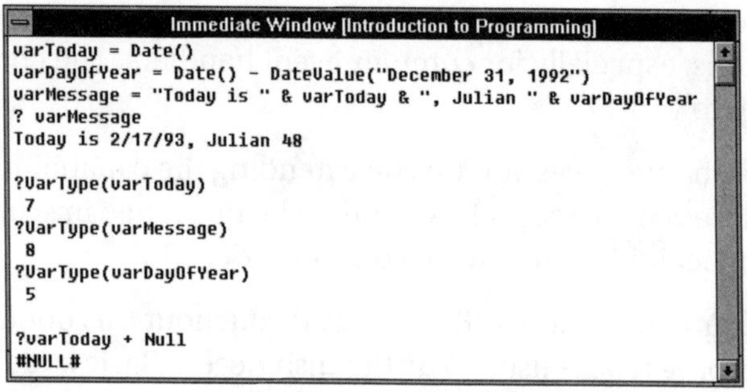

```
Immediate Window [Introduction to Programming]
varToday = Date()
varDayOfYear = Date() - DateValue("December 31, 1992")
varMessage = "Today is " & varToday & ", Julian " & varDayOfYear
? varMessage
Today is 2/17/93, Julian 48

?VarType(varToday)
 7
?VarType(varMessage)
 8
?VarType(varDayOfYear)
 5

?varToday + Null
#NULL#
```

Fig. 10.1 *The Immediate Window displaying Access Basic code examples.*

Note: Prefix Immediate Window statements that return values with ?. (The ? symbol is shorthand for Print.) Values are returned on the line following the ? statement. If you forget the ?, you receive the message `Expected: statement`.

Add Option Explicit to every module you create to prevent errors

Add the `Option Explicit` instruction to the Declarations section of your modules. Option Explicit requires that you declare variables with the `Dim` instruction before you use them in your code. Explicitly declaring variables before you use them is a good programming practice and prevents errors that arise from typing errors when you enter variable names in your code.

Like xBase and PAL, Access Basic enables you to declare *ad hoc* variables by giving a value to a name with the = operator. Although the capability to create ad hoc variables appears to simplify writing code, you pay the price when debugging your applications; if you accidentally enter `cmbPickLust` rather than `cmbPickList`, Access creates `cmbPickLust` for you rather than generates a `Can't find cmbPickLust` error message. `cmbPickLust` always has the default value 0, but your code expects it to return the last value assigned to `cmbPickList`. This type of error is difficult to spot, especially if you use long variable names.

Another advantage of declaring your variables is eliminating the necessity of using BASIC's type declaration characters, such as `$` and `%`, in variable names. When you declare your variables with `Dim` *VarName* `As` *VarType*, all instances of *VarName* are of *VarType*, and you don't need to add the type declaration character. Numeric variables are assigned the value 0, and string variables are empty (the equivalent of *VarName* = `""`, sometimes called a *null string*). The `Null` value, discussed in a later tip, is different than 0 and the empty or "null" string.

Note: If you declare a variable without adding **As** *VarType*, the variable is created as an uninitialized **Variant** data type. The following tip discusses some of the special properties of the **Variant** data type.

Concatenate different types of data with the Variant data type

Access Basic and Visual Basic 2.0 introduce the **Variant** type to the BASIC language. You can use **Variant** types to hold values of data cells of tables and queries, and to create composite indexes on fields of more than one data type.

The primary advantage of the **Variant** data type in Access Basic code is that you can concatenate (combine) variables of different data types without first using functions, such as **Str$**(), to explicitly convert a number or a date to a string. Thus, the instruction

```
varMessage = "Today is " & varToday & ", Julian "
& varDayOfYear
```

is perfectly legal if varToday and varDayOfYear are **Variant** types. The equivalent statement in xBase, another dialect of BASIC, requires two functions to convert the date and number values to a string before concatenation:

```
Message = "Today is " + DTOS(Today) + ", Julian "
+ STR(DayOfYear)
```

Note: Variables of the **Variant** data type can return a type integer that defines the nature of the data they contain. **VarType**(*varName*) returns 0 if *varName* has been declared (with **Dim**) but not initialized with a value. Uninitialized **Variant** variables return 0. Later tips note other type integers for variables of the **Variant** data type.

Use Access Basic's & operator, not +, to concatenate values

When you use operators to concatenate variables, use the & operator rather than the + operator to avoid ambiguity in concatenation. If, for example, you try to concatenate two **Variant** types that contain numeric values, such as 123 and 456, with the + symbol the result is 579; **&**, on the other hand, gives the desired result, 123456. Also use **&** rather than + for the following reasons:

- **&** is the standard concatenation symbol used in SQL statements.

- Concatenating a variable having the **Null** value with a numeric or date variable using + results in **Null**, not the number or the date.

Use prefix variable names to make your code easier to read

Hungarian notation—traditionally used to identify the data type of variable in C programming—is equally useful in Access Basic and other dialects of Microsoft Object Basic, such as Visual Basic. Use, for example, the prefix *var* for variables of the **Variant** data type, *db* for database objects, *tbl* for table objects, and so forth. Using a prefix that represents the data type makes your code easier to read and thus easier to debug.

Note: The term Hungarian notation derives from the birthplace of the originator of the convention, Charles Simonyi, and the probability that only Hungarians can pronounce *lpsz* (long pointer to a zero-terminated string), a prefix for string variable names in the C language.

Eliminate case sensitivity from text comparisons

When you create a new module, Access adds the line `Option Compare Database` to your Declarations section. This statement causes text data comparisons to be made based on the sequence of the characters' position in the sorting table in use (ANSI for the U.S. version of Access). As a result, the text comparisons are case sensitive.

To eliminate case sensitivity from text comparisons, change `Option Compare Database` to `Option Compare Text` to eliminate the need to use `UCase()` or `UCase$()` functions in statements such as

```
If UCase$(lpstrString1) = UCase$(lpstrString2)
Then
    [code to be executed]
End If
```

Using `Option Compare Text` can save a good deal of typing if you have many text comparisons in your code.

Use a simple Access Basic function to enable users to quit Access

The main entry form of your application usually includes a command button, Quit, that enables the user to close the form and quit Access at the same time. You want the user to confirm that he or she wants to quit with a message box. If the user clicks the No button, you invoke the CancelEvent action.

The user, however, may decide to quit by double-clicking the document control box or choosing Close from the document control menu. If you attach a macro with the Quit action to the OnPush event of the command button and the OnClose event of the form to handle both methods of closing the form, the message box appears twice when you click the Quit button, because quitting Access closes open forms and the message box appears in response to the OnClose event. A simple Access Basic function, ThreeWayQuit, solves this problem:

```
Function ThreeWayQuit (FromButton As Integer)
    'Quits Access from button or Document Control
        Box with message box
    'Pass 0 as argument from the OnClose event
        (=ThreeWayQuit(False))
    'Pass -1 as argument from the OnPush event
        (=ThreeWayQuit(True))
    'Error trapping is required for DoCmd Close
        action cancellation
    On Error Resume Next   'Turn off error
        messages
    If wFromButton Then
        DoCmd Close A_FORM, "Main Switchboard"
    Else
        If MsgBox("Are you sure you want to
          quit?", 36) = 6 Then
            DoCmd Quit
        Else
            DoCmd CancelEvent
        End If
    End If
    On Error GoTo 0   'Resume error messages
End Function
```

To demonstrate this function, open the Main Switchboard form in Design mode and enter **=ThreeWayQuit(True)** as the OnPush event handler for the Quit command button. Add **=ThreeWayQuit(False)** to the OnClose event text box of the form. Change to Run mode and click the Quit button; then choose Yes in the message box that appears. Relaunch Access and try double-clicking the document control box or choose Close from the document control menu.

Note: The name of this macro is derived from the Cantonese delicacy Four-Way Duck, also known as The Same Duck Served Four Ways.

Employ user-defined functions to simplify domain integrity validation

 If your form has many fields, the macros required to enforce domain integrity can become quite lengthy. In Access Basic, you can use complex structures, such as **Select Case...End Case** statements (not available with macros), to perform the tests. With Access Basic, you can use a single **MsgBox** command with the text of the message determined by the error. Better yet, you can set the focus to the control object that needs a correcting entry.

To use an Access Basic function to test for domain integrity when adding a new record, enter =*ValidationFn*( ) to the BeforeUpdate event of the form. Then create a validation function with a structure similar to the following:

```
Function ValidationFn()
    Dim wBadValue As Integer
    Dim lpstrMsg As String
    If InStr(Forms!FormName!Field1, "ValidList")
      = 0 Then
        wBadValue = True
        lpstrMsg = "Bad value in Field1."
        DoCmd GoToControl "Field1"
    End If
    Select Case Forms!FormName!Field2
        Case "A Good Value"
        Case "Another Good Value"
        Case Else
            wBadValue = True
            lpstrMsg = "Bad value in Field2."
            DoCmd GoToControl "Field2"
    End Select
    [code that tests other fields]
    If wBadValue Then
        MsgBox lpstrMsg, 16
        DoCmd CancelEvent
    End If
End Function
```

Create a library database for Access Basic utility functions

As you develop new applications, you should find that you create other general-purpose functions that have across-the-board applicability. Save each of these functions in a module of a database named Utility Library or the like, and then import the functions from the library module when you need them. Alternatively, you can copy the code for the function to the Clipboard and then paste the code into a text file that you create with Windows Notepad. Then select the code you want in Notepad and copy the selection to the Clipboard. Paste the code into your module to add the library function.

IsLoaded( ), the function Microsoft forgot to include as an intrinsic Access Basic function, is a good candidate for a module in a library database. You can copy IsLoaded( ) from NWIND.MDB's Introduction to Programming module to the Clipboard and then paste it into the IsLoaded module you create in your library database. Almost every application needs to use the IsLoaded( ) function at some point to determine whether a form whose name is passed as an argument is open. You can use, for example, the Not IsLoaded( ) as a condition of a macro action to open the form whose name is passed as IsLoaded( )'s argument.

Use Access Basic code to document your applications

Access provides no direct provision to document the macros you write. The macro argument fields of Database Analyzer's @MacroDetails table includes integer values for values you select from a list box. The Access documentation or help file doesn't include how these values translate to menu names or other verbs and nouns. (Some of these macro values are discussed in the tip "Use the A_ action constants with DoMenuItem and macro arguments" later in the chapter.)

If you write Access Basic code to substitute for macro actions, you can save your code as an ANSI text file and then print the code to document your application. With your module open in Design mode, choose File Save Text and then enter the file name in the Save Text dialog. (By default, Access uses the first eight letters, up to the first space, of the module's name.)

Note: Use Notepad to print your code. Notepad adds the file name as the header and the page number as a footer. Be sure to choose Edit Word Wrap so that lines longer than about 80 characters aren't truncated. If you use a word processor for printing code, use a monospace font, such as Courier, so that indenting and other formatting appears as in the Module window.

Make code easier to read by reducing the indentation tab width

Code with many nested If…Then structures becomes difficult to read in the Module window and on the printed page. You need to use the horizontal scroll bar in the Module window to read the indented code, and the majority of lines wrap to the left margins on code printouts. You can reduce the severity of this problem by changing the default tab stops used to indent code from 4 characters to 3 or even 2 characters. Choose View Options and then select Module Design in the Categories list box. Set the value of the Tab Stop Width property to 3 or 2.

Use sub-procedures to segment complex functions

Most Access Basic functions you write are quite short. If you write complex functions, you can make your code more readable and easier to debug if you move blocks of code that perform different operations into individual sub-procedures. Sub-procedures are **Sub** *ProcName*…**End Sub** structures in Access.

Use the **Call** *ProcName* instruction to run sub-procedures so that procedure calls are clearly identified. If you use only the sub-procedure name to call the sub-procedure—which is allowed in Access Basic—you may confuse the sub-procedure name with a variable name.

Note: Enclose arguments passed to sub-procedures within parentheses when you use the **Call** instruction, as in **Call** *ProcName* (*Argument1*, *Argument2*, …). Parentheses aren't used if you omit the **Call** instruction.

Use the A_ action constants with DoMenuItem and macro arguments

Access Basic includes a set of predeclared (intrinsic) symbolic constants for some arguments of macro actions that you select from combo boxes. Each constant begins with A_; the name of a menu bar or choice, or another argument follows the underscore, as in A_FILE for the File menu bar. Using intrinsic constant names rather than their corresponding numeric values makes your code easier to read.

Some constants are described in the Access documentation; see the DoMenuItem entry in the *Language Reference* as an example. The Access help system provides an alphabetic "laundry list" of the A_ constants. (Search help for *constants*.) The help list is of little help, however, because the constants aren't organized by the action to which they apply.

Only part of the selections from macro action argument combo boxes have predeclared constants. If the constant you need isn't on the list, you need to open a Macro window and then open the combo box for argument. The

numeric value you use for the argument of the action in
Access basic is the position of the value in the combo box
list, counting from 0 as the position of the first argument
in the list.

Add the DoEvents instruction to loops to prevent computer lockups

Accidental *infinite loops* you create in Access Basic lock up
your computer and require a warm boot (Alt+Ctrl+Delete)
to recover. An infinite loop is a **Do...Loop** or **For...Next** structure in which the instruction that causes the loop to end is
never executed. (The only case in which a **For...Next** loop
executes indefinitely is when you modify the value of the
loop counter by code within the loop. Doing so isn't a
good programming practice.)

To avoid locking up your computer, insert a **DoEvents** instruction after the **Do** instruction. **DoEvents** tests to determine whether any messages—such as a Ctrl+Break key
combination to stop execution of your code—are in the
Windows message queue. If messages are waiting,
DoEvents allows the messages to be processed before the
next loop is executed. You can remove the **DoEvents** instruction so that your application runs faster after you test
your code thoroughly.

Create queries with the CreateQueryDef( ) method

Chapter 7 includes a tip, "Work around fixed RowSource
properties of combo and list boxes," that shows how to
change the query for the RowSource property to fill
combo boxes with different values. A more elegant solution to the "locked RowSource property" problem is to
create changeable queries by using Access Basic's

`CreateQueryDef`() method. Following is an example of the code you need to create a new query:

```
Function RowSourceQuery ()
    'Declare object variables
    Dim dbNwind As Database, qdfQuery As QueryDef
    Set dbNwind = CurrentDB()

    'Delete an existing "RowSource Query" query
      definition, if one exists
    On Error Resume Next
    dbNwind.DeleteQueryDef ("RowSource Query")
    On Error GoTo 0

    'Create a new query definition
    Set qdfQuery =
      dbNwind.CreateQueryDef("RowSource Query")

    'Send the Access Basic SQL statement
    qdfQuery.SQL = "SELECT * FROM Suppliers WHERE
      [Supplier ID] < 11;"
End Function
```

Attach this function to an action, such as the OnPush property of a command button, to choose the query you want. You can pass all or a portion of the SQL statement to the function as the value of an argument, as in =**RowSourceQuery** ("WHERE [Supplier ID] < 11"). In this case, your SQL statement would be

```
qdfQuery.SQL = "SELECT * FROM Suppliers " &
lpszSQL & ";"
```

assuming the header of your function is `Function` RowSourceQuery (lpszSQL `As String`).

Note: You can combine the `.CreateQueryDef`() method and **.SQL** property into a single instruction by adding the SQL statement as an argument of `.CreateQueryDef`(), as in db*Database*.**CreateQueryDef**(*QueryName*, *SQLStatement*). Using the two instructions separately, however, makes your code easier to understand.

Use Snapshots to preserve values in multiuser environments

Data in Access tables or updatable queries may change as a result of append or edit operations performed by others in the same Access workgroup. If, for example, you are printing a report based on a Dynaset, and another user changes a value in a table included in your Dynaset, totals in your report may not correspond to the sum of the values in the totaled rows. This problem, often called a *cross-footing error*, results from the multiple-pass report generation process used by Access; totals are calculated before your report starts printing.

To solve the problem, use the `CreateSnapshot()` method to create a Snapshot that is an image of the data in the table or query at the time you take the Snapshot. Then base your report on the name Snapshot (using the name of the Snapshot) rather than a Dynaset.

Use the Seek method to speed table lookup operations

Use the `Seek` method to locate records based on values of indexed table fields. One advantage of using Access Basic is that you can control which index of a multiple-indexed table is active with the **.Index** property.

Note: You cannot use the `OpenTable()` method to open a table in an attached database. The `OpenTable()` method is restricted to tables in Access .MDB databases. Thus, you cannot use the `Seek` method on a table in an attached database. Use the `CreateDynaset()` method to open a table attached from database, using a statement of the type `dbAttached.CreateDynaset("TableName")`.

The **.Index** property of table objects is similar to the SET INDEX TO command of xBase. You can set the index to the index created automatically when you specify a primary key with a `tblTableName`.**Index** = `"PrimaryKey"` instruction. You specify composite indexes with the instruction `tblTableName`.**Index** = `"Index#"`, where *Index#* is chosen from `Index1…Index5`. Indexes on single fields other than the primary key field are specified by the field name, as in `tblTableName`.**Index** = `"FieldName"`.

Note: The **Seek** method applies only to Table objects. You cannot perform a **Seek** on a query, Dynaset, or Snapshot.

The **Seek** method of Access Basic is more flexible than the SEEK command of xBase. You use the =, >=, >, <=, or < operators to specify the record you want to find, with the value you are seeking. In most cases, you use the = operator with the value you are seeking, as in `tblTableName`.**Seek** `"="`, `"SoughtValue"`. If the index on the specified field permits duplicate values, the **Seek** method returns the first match it finds. If the **Seek** method doesn't find a matching value, the **NoMatch** property of the table is set to **True**.

NoMatch = **True** is equivalent to xBase's EOF( ), and **NoMatch** = **False** represents the xBase FOUND( ) function. If you make a composite primary key, or if an `Index1…Index5` instruction indexes the active index, add the values of each indexed field in sequence as arguments of the **Seek** method:

```
tblTableName.Seek "=", "Index1Value",
"Index2Value", …
```

The **Seek** method for data in tables is faster than the **FindFirst** method, especially when you have a large number of records in the table. Speed differences between **Seek** and **FindFirst** in Access are similar to the relative performance of SEEK and FIND in xBase.

Note: The Access 1.0 documentation is inconsistent regarding the syntax used to specify index names that include spaces or punctuation symbols. *Don't* add square brackets when you specify an index name. *Don't* add a space between Primary and Key when you specify the primary key index.

Test for relational integrity with Access Basic code

Setting the default relationships between tables by choosing Edit Relationships and marking the Enforce Referential Integrity check box results in an error message if you try to violate referential integrity rules in an append, edit, or delete operation on one of the tables. As a result, you may want to provide a message box that provides a more explicit warning to users of your applications.

Use the **Seek** method on the primary key of the base table when adding entries in related tables to verify that the foreign key value entered in a related table has a corresponding value in the primary key of the base table. Similarly, test for records in the related table with values equal to the primary key before you try to delete a record in the base table. In the latter case, you can add code to perform a cascade delete if the user confirms the deletion.

Following is an example of generic Access Basic code that combines a referential integrity test with an optional cascade delete:

```
Function TestRelTable()
    Dim dbDatabase As Database
    Set dbDatabase = CurrentDB()
    Dim tblTableName As Table
    Set tblTableName =
      dbDatabase.OpenTable("TableName")
```

```
Dim lpstrKeyValue As Control
Set lpstrKeyValue =
    Forms!FormName!PrimaryKeyTextBox

tblTableName.Index = "ForeignKeyField"
tblTableName.Seek "=", lpstrKeyValue

If Not tblTableName.NoMatch Then
    If MsgBox("OK to delete message",36) = 6
      Then
        Do While Not tblTableName.NoMatch
            DoEvents 'temporary
            tblTableName.Seek "=",
              lpstrKeyValue
            If Not tblTableName.NoMatch Then
                tblTableName.Delete
            End If
        Loop
    End If
End If
tblTableName.Close
dbDatabase.Close
End Function
```

Use transaction processing to speed updates with multiple edits

Processing a large number of individual updates to tables or queries with the Update method slows down your application. You can accelerate updates, however, by using multiple edits. You can speed up bulk deletions, for instance, by using the **BeginTrans…CommitTrans¦Rollback** statements, as in the following example (derived from the code in the preceding tip):

```
If Not tblTableName.NoMatch Then
    BeginTrans
    On Error GoTo DoRollback
    Do While Not tblTableName.NoMatch
        DoEvents 'temporary
        tblTableName.Seek "=", lpstrKeyValue
```

```
                If Not tblTableName.NoMatch Then
                    tblTableName.Delete
                End If
            Loop
            If MsgBox("OK to delete message",36) = 6
            Then
                CommitTrans
            Else
DoRollback:
                If Err <> 0 Then
                    MsgBox "Unable to perform
                        deletion.", 48
                End If
                Rollback
            End If
        End If
        On Error GoTo 0
```

The deletions performed within the **Do While...Loop** structure, preceded by the **BeginTrans** statement, aren't made
permanent until execution of the **CommitTrans** statement. If
you execute the **Rollback** command, all changes are dis-
carded.

Extend Access Basic's capabilities
with Windows API and DLL functions

Windows 3.1 includes more than 500 functions that you
can call on to extend the capabilities of Access Basic. The
major hurdle isn't writing the code to use the function, but
finding the name of the right function to do the job. Use
the FindWindow() function to determine whether a particular Windows application is running.

You can use the common dialog functions of Windows 3.1
to choose binary or other special-purpose files to open
and save. The FileOpen common dialog, for example, can
replace the simple **InputBox$()** function in the ReadBLOB()
function of the preceding tip. Similarly, you can use the

FileSave common dialog to choose a file name to save data in the **WriteBLOB()** function.

To make full use of the Windows API functions, you need a copy of the documentation that accompanies the Windows 3.1 Software Development Kit (SDK). You can buy only the documentation portion of the SDK directly from Microsoft Corp. or from many technical bookstores. Microsoft Visual C++ and Borland International's C++ compilers also include full documentation for the Windows 3.1 API. If you have a CD-ROM drive, you can obtain the documentation in the form of WinHelp files on the CD-ROMs distributed through the Microsoft Developer Network.

You can use third-party commercial, freeware, and shareware DLLs to add to your applications specialized features not included in Access. Your Access Basic code can call the functions in most DLLs written for Visual Basic. You cannot use Visual Basic custom controls (.VBX files), however, with Access. Thus, Visual Basic DLLs that rely on Visual Basic custom controls aren't suitable for use with Access Basic.

Use Visual Basic's WIN30API.TXT for function prototype declarations

When you use functions of a Windows or third-party DLL in your code, you first need to declare the function prototype in the Declarations section of your module. Typing function prototype declarations, however, is a long and tedious process. You can save a great deal of time and frustration by copying the function prototype declarations you need from WIN30API.TXT and WIN31EXT.TXT, and then pasting the prototype code into the declarations section of your module. These two text files are included with Visual Basic 2.0.

The following prototype for the `GetPrivateProfileString()`
and `WritePrivateProfileString()` functions of Windows
3.1 is typical of these declarations:

```
Declare Function GetPrivateProfileString
   Lib "Kernel"
     (ByVal lpApplicationName As String,
      ByVal lpKeyName As String,
      ByVal lpDefault As String,
      ByVal lpReturnedString As String,
      ByVal nSize As Integer,
      ByVal lpFileName As String) As Integer

Declare Function WritePrivateProfileString Lib
   "Kernel"
     (ByVal lpApplicationName As String,
      ByVal lpKeyName As String,
      ByVal lpString As String,
      ByVal lpFileName As String) As Integer
```

Note: The entire declaration must be on one line in your
Access Basic code, not on multiple lines as in the preceding example. Explanations usually stack the arguments of
the function in the manner shown for readability.

The keyword **Lib** indicates the name of the DLL that contains the function—in this case KERNEL.EXE, one of the
DLLs of Windows 3.x. The **ByVal** keyword causes variables
to be passed by value, rather than by reference, to the DLL
function.

Note: If you don't have Visual Basic, you can download
W31API.ZIP from the Visual Basic for Windows library (5)
of the MSBASIC forum on CompuServe. To make the process simpler, download the API Helper (AH02.ZIP) from
the same forum. API Helper is a Visual Basic application
that enables you to choose the API function you want
from a list and copy the function to the Clipboard.

Use Windows API functions to read data from private .INI files

You can read from or write to the private initialization (.INI) files that well-behaved Windows applications create on installation. These private .INI files substitute for entries in WIN.INI. Private .INI files often contain a wealth of information about the operating parameters of Windows applications. MSACCESS.INI is typical of private .INI files used by Windows applications. You can create, for example, functions that return the file name of and path to the SYSTEM.MDA file now used by an Access application with the following Access Basic code that reads MSACCESS.INI:

```
Function lpstrReadIni ()
    Dim nSize As Integer
    Dim nLength As Integer
    lpstrFile = "msaccess.ini"
    lpstrSection = "Options"
    lpstrLine = "SystemDB"
    lpstrDefault = "system.mda"
    lpstrData = Space$(128)
    nSize = Len(lpstrData)
    nLength = GetPrivateProfileString
            (lpstrSection, lpstrLine,
             lpstrDefault, lpstrData,
             nSize, lpstrFile)
    lpstrReadIni = UCase$(Left$(lpstrData,
            nLength))
End Function
```

Note: To use the lpstrReadIni() function, you need to declare the GetPrivateProfileString() function with the statement shown in the preceding tip, and the variables lpstrFile, lpstrSection, lpstrLine, lpstrDefault, and lpstrData with the **Dim...As String** statement in the Declarations section of your module.

The line `lpstrData` = **Space$**(128) creates a *buffer* (position in memory) to hold the data returned by `GetPrivateProfileString()`. The four lines beginning with `nLength` = must appear on one line in your code. The `lpstrReadIni()` function returns the string following `SystemDB=` in the [Options] section). Thus, you can use =`lpstrReadIni()` to set the value of the Control Source property of a list box and display the user's current system database.

Note: The prefix `lpstr` of `lpstrReadIni()` indicates that the function returns a pointer to an Access string. Strings in Access aren't zero-terminated strings (`lpsz`); the **ByVal** keyword, used in arguments for DLL function calls, converts the Access `lpstr` strings to C's `lpsz` or `lp` string.

Make changes to MSACCESS.INI with WritePrivateProfileString( )

You can change the entry for `SystemDB=` in the MSACCESS.INI file with code similar to that shown in the preceding tip. In this case, pass the string containing the new path and file name for SYSTEM.MDA as the value of the argument, `lpstrData`, to a function that calls the Windows `WritePrivateProfileString()` function.

```
Function wWriteIni (lpstrData As String)
    lpstrFile = "msaccess.ini"
    lpstrSection = "Options"
    lpstrLine = "SystemDB"
    wWriteIni = WritePrivateProfileString
                (lpstrSection, lpstrLine,
                 lpstrData, lpstrFile)
End Function
```

The `wWriteIni()` function returns a non-zero number if successful or 0 (False) if the function cannot make the change. You can run `wWriteIni()` from the OnPush event of a command button (=**wWriteIni(**"*SystemDBFile*")), as the condition of a macro (**If Not wWriteIni** ("*SystemDBFile*")), or as the argument of a RunCode macro action RunCode **wWriteIni**("*SystemDBFile*").

You need to close and relaunch Access for the changes you make to MSACCESS.INI to become effective.

Note: The variable names you use for arguments when you call the declared function need not correspond to the argument names in the function prototype declaration. Argument names in function prototype declarations are only placeholders for the argument type declarations.

Use Visual Basic code to import functions to Access modules

You can use most of the declarations and procedure code contained in Visual Basic .BAS files and the event-handling code included in .FRM files in your Access Basic modules. Importing special-purpose user-defined functions and standard procedures in Visual Basic into your Access Basic code can save you a great deal of time.

You can download a vast amount of Visual Basic code for a wide range of applications from the Visual Basic/Win Library of the MSACCESS Forum on CompuServe. Much of this Visual Basic code contains functions and procedures that are quite useful in Access Basic modules.

Use Visual Basic to save the code to a text file; then import the text file into your Access Basic module. You will need to modify or delete the event-handling procedures associated with forms. Many Visual Basic applications have been *ported* (converted) to Access Basic code.

Note: While you make the necessary changes to the code, turn syntax checking off by choosing View Options, selecting the Module Design category, and setting the value of

the Syntax Checking property to No. After you finish your
changes and verify that your code will compile in Access
Basic (**Run Compile All**), turn syntax checking on.

11

Networking Access

Microsoft Access includes many features that enhance your ability to share Access databases with others in a multiuser environment. Access is equally at home on simple peer-to-peer networks such as Windows for Workgroups, LANtastic, and NetWare Lite, and on client-server networks such as Novell NetWare, Microsoft LAN Manager, and Banyan Vines. Access includes a complete security system, modeled on the security system of Microsoft SQL Server, a client-server database system that now runs under OS/2.

This chapter provides tips on how to make the most effective use of Access on a network, with emphasis on how to create the secure database systems you need when you share your Access applications.

Note: Workgroup information is stored in the SYSTEM.MDA file shared by workgroup members. The SYSTEM.MDA file, discussed throughout this chapter, contains information about the account for each member. An *account* consists of the user's logon name, four-digit personal identification number (PIN), and password. Access combines the user's logon name and PIN into a Security ID (SID) value stored in the MSysAccounts table of SYSTEM.MDA. PINs are used to distinguish between two users with the same logon name.

Use the Show System Objects option to view System Information

All Access databases contain a number of tables with names that begin with MSys. These tables maintain records with information on database objects. Some fields of these tables depend on information contained in the particular copy of SYSTEM.MDA attached to Access when you or another user created the objects. You can examine the content of the system tables of your database by choosing View Options and then setting the value of the Show System Objects property to Yes.

Some system tables are secure; you receive the message `No permissions for 'MSysColumns'` if you try to open, for example, the MSysColumns table. This message is the same one users receive if they try to open a table or other object for which they don't have Read Data permission. Choose Security Permissions and then assign yourself Read Data permission on tables for which that check box isn't marked.

Don't change the data in any system table. If you make changes to the data, you may find that you cannot open a database object or alter a control object on a form or report.

Note: You can see a list of all tables in SYSTEM.MDA and import or attach SYSTEM.MDA tables, such as Access Preferences and MSysAccounts, that aren't included in the list when you Show System Objects, if you are a member of the Admins group. Choose File Import to open the Import dialog. Then choose Microsoft Access as the Data source and click OK. In the Select Microsoft Access Database dialog, enter **system.mda** in the File Name text box and click OK. In the Import Objects dialog, choose Tables as the Object Type and then pick, for example, the MSysAccounts table to import. Open the MSysAccounts table to display the group and user accounts for the copy of SYSTEM.MDA in your \ACCESS directory.

Grant limited permissions to enable workgroups to attach shared tables

You can enable members of one workgroup (such as Sales) to obtain data from tables located in databases shared by another workgroup (such as Personnel) by attaching the Personnel tables to the Sales workgroup's database(s). Access normally enables you to open only one database at a time, although you can open more than one database with Access Basic code.

Members of the Personnel workgroup likely will limit availability of confidential data contained in personnel files, such as salary and performance review information, to other workgroups. The Personnel department also is unlikely to allow other workgroups to change the accessible data. Thus, the database administrator of the Personnel department will grant permissions to users in the Sales department to attach designated tables of the Personnel database to the Sales database as read-only objects.

The database administrator of the foreign database (Personnel) must add the logon name and PIN of each user of another workgroup (Sales) who needs to attach tables to the Users group of Personnel's SYSTEM.MDA file. Members of the Sales group need Read Data permissions from Personnel tables that are attached to the Sales workgroup's database(s).

Note: The preceding paragraph applies only to attaching tables from foreign Access databases. The database administrator or owner of the client-server database grants permissions to attach tables of client-server RDBMS. Use the security features of your network operating system to restrict permissions for dBASE, FoxBASE, Paradox, and Btrieve tables.

Save yourself headaches by keeping a permanent record of all PINs

You need to know a user's PIN to re-create an account for the user if the SYSTEM.MDA that contains the user's account is corrupted or lost. Administrators of other workgroup databases need the PIN number of users to whom they grant privileges to attach tables. Keep the list of logon names and PIN numbers in a secure area to prevent unauthorized access to this information. Be sure to duplicate the case of letters in logon names. Although logon names aren't case-sensitive for the purpose of logging on to Access, the case of the characters in logon names is used to create the SID (system ID) for each user account.

Keep data secure by encouraging users to change passwords regularly

Encourage users to change their passwords periodically to improve database security. Monthly or quarterly password changes are the norm in many organizations. To change a password, follow these steps:

1. Choose Security Change Password to display the Change Password dialog.

2. Enter the old password, the new password, and then the new password again for confirmation. (Remember that passwords are case sensitive.)

Note: When you enter the first password, use the Tab key to bypass the Old Password text box. Access assigns you, the Admin user, an empty (blank) password as the default.

After you enter a password, you must log onto Access by entering your user name (Admin, if you haven't changed it) and your password.

Use the SystemDB= line to determine your Access workgroup

The line beginning with `SystemDB=` in the `[Options]` section of your MSACCESS.INI file determines the location and name of the SYSTEM.MDA file for your workgroup. Depending on the type of network used, you specify the drive designator and full path, such as **e:\access\system.mda**, or use ***ServerName**Directory*\system.mda** to locate the SYSTEM.MDA file for the workgroup.

Each workgroup member requires a personal copy of MSACCESS.INI in the local default Windows directory (the directory in which WIN.COM is located). When you launch Access, if your Windows files and MSACCESS.EXE are located on the local disk drive or in network server directories, Access first checks the local default Windows directory for the presence of MSACCESS.INI to determine initialization parameters, including the location of SYSTEM.MDA.

Use STFSETUP.EXE /W to change your workgroup

In the directory where your MSACCESS.EXE file is stored is the Access Setup application, STFSETUP.EXE. After you install Access, the purpose of STFSETUP.EXE is to change the value of the `SystemDB=` line in the `[Options]` group of MSACCESS.INI. The `SystemDB=` line specifies the path and file name of the system library that Access automatically attaches when started.

If you are a member of a workgroup and sharing a SYSTEM.MDA located on a server, the entry may appear similar to `SystemDB=d:\system.mda`. The system file may have any name the workgroup administrator wants to give it, as long as its location, relative to your computer, and file name appear in the `SystemDB=` line.

To change your workgroup, double-click the Workgroups icon to access the Microsoft Access Change Workgroup application. STFSETUP.EXE displays the Specify Workgroup dialog. Enter the full path and name of the system database file for the workgroup you want to join.

Note: Changing workgroups with STFSETUP.EXE doesn't change the working directory to the new location of SYSTEM.MDA you specify. Specify the new drive and/or directory of the new workgroup database in the Open Database dialog when you join a new workgroup.

If you have deleted the Microsoft Access Change Workgroup application with other marginal members of the Access program group, you can re-create the Workgroups icon by following these steps:

1. Select the program group in which the Access icon is located.

2. In Program Manager, choose File New.

3. In the New Program Object dialog, click the Program Item option button (if it isn't selected), and then choose OK.

4. In the Program Item Properties dialog, enter **Workgroups** in the Description text box and **c:\access\stfsetup /w** in the Command Line text box.

   Note: If STFSETUP.EXE is located in a different directory than listed in the preceding example, add the correct directory to the path in the Command Line text box.

5. Choose OK.

Note: In Chapter 10, the tip "Make changes to MSACCESS.INI with WritePrivateProfileString()" describes how you can add the capability to change workgroups within an Access application by adding only a few lines of Access Basic code. Before you change `SystemDB=` with `WritePrivateProfileString()`, however, add a few more lines of code to test for the existence of the file corresponding to the file name and path you specify.

Substitute more descriptive names for SYSTEM.MDA files

You don't need to use SYSTEM.MDA to identify the system database for every workgroup. You can use more descriptive names, such as SALES.MDA or CREDIT.MDA, if you enter the name and location of the system database in the `SystemDB=` line under `[Options]` in the MSACCESS.INI files of all workgroup members.

Check the SystemDB= entry in MSACCESS.INI if you can't run Access

If your `SystemDB=` entry of MSACCESS.INI points to a system database file that Access cannot open (because the file doesn't exist or because you aren't logged onto the network), Access displays a message such as `'E:\ACCESS'` `is not a valid path`. When you choose OK, Access stops abruptly. This problem also can occur if you change the drive designator on your computer for the shared server directory that contains the workgroup system file.

When you encounter this problem, launch STFSETUP.EXE (as discussed earlier in "Use STFSETUP.EXE /W to change your workgroup") and change the path to correspond to the location of the system library file you want to use. Then try launching Access again.

Note: Absence of a `SystemDB=` entry in MSACCESS.INI causes Access to check the current working directory (shown in Program Manager's Program Item Properties dialog for your Access icon) for SYSTEM.MDA. If Access finds SYSTEM.MDA in the working directory, Access will run.

Enable all users to use a customized UTILITY.MDA file

UTILITY.MDA is an Access library that contains various components needed to run the retail version of Access, such as the forms that comprise the toolbars and the form for the Zoom box. All users, regardless of the workgroup to which they belong, can share a common UTILITY.MDA file.

If you create custom toolbars or change the font for the Zoom box (using methods described in the next chapter), you may want all workgroup members to be able to use the modified version of UTILITY.MDA. Change the `UtilityDB=` line of the `[Options]` section of MSACCESS.INI to point to the location of the single UTILITY.MDA file.

Note: Access will stop just as abruptly as described in the preceding tip if it cannot find the utility database you specify in the `UtilityDB=` line. If you delete the `UtilityDB=` line, Access looks for a file named UTILITY.MDA in the working directory.

Avoid locking yourself out of your database by backing up database files

A *database system* is defined as a combination of SYSTEM.MDA and the databases created while that copy of SYSTEM.MDA was attached to your copy of Access. Back up all the database files you created and the SYSTEM.MDA file(s) that you used when you created or modified the .MDB files before you implement security provisions, such as deleting the Admin user account or encrypting your database files. This way, if you make an error in establishing database security and lock yourself out of your own database applications, you can restore them, together with the SYSTEM.MDA file(s), and return to square one.

Finalize database security by deleting the Admin user

The first step in establishing a secure database system is to add a new account for yourself in the Admins group, and then delete the Admin user. To add your new account, follow these steps:

1. Choose Security Users to open the Users dialog. Click the New button to open the New User/Group dialog.

2. Enter your new user name and PIN in the Name and Personal ID Number text boxes and write both entries in your Users log. Then click OK to return to the Users dialog.

3. Select the Admins group in the Available Groups list box, and then click the Add >> button. Choose Close to return to Access's main window.

You are added to the Users group. After you add your new account, follow these steps to delete the Admin user:

1. Close and relaunch Access.

2. Log in with the new user name and assign yourself a password.

3. Close and relaunch Access again, and then test your new logon name and password. If Access doesn't accept your new identity, enter **Admin** and a blank

password, and then review the entry for your logon name.

4. After you open Access with your new account, check to see that you can open each object in the database files you have created in Design mode. This step ensures that you have Modify Definitions permissions for all objects.

5. If the test in step 4 is successful, select the Admin user in the Users dialog and delete the Admin account. If the test isn't successful, don't delete the Admin account until you find out why you cannot modify your own objects.

Save a clean copy of SYSTEM.MDA after you delete the Admin user

Make a backup copy of SYSTEM.MDA after you add your new account as a member of the Admins and Users groups and delete the Admin user. Use this copy to create new SYSTEM.MDA files for other workgroups, if you haven't created any Access applications for workgroups. (If you have created workgroup applications before establishing system security, see the later tip "Prevent Admins from having irrevocable permissions.") A clean copy of SYSTEM.MDA eliminates the need for deleting the Admin user account and adding your own account each time you create a new workgroup.

Keep your Access distribution diskettes in a safe place

Keeping your Access installation diskettes in a safe place is a good idea. If your SYSTEM.MDA file becomes corrupted or disappears and you don't have a backup copy, you need to re-create the SYSTEM.MDA file by reinstalling Access from the original installation diskettes.

Note: Groups, as well as users, have a SecurityID (SID) value. Access creates a unique SID for the Admins group based on the Company and User Name you enter when you install Access, plus the serial number of the first installation diskette. If an unauthorized person obtains your distribution diskettes, he or she can install a copy of Access that has the same Admins group SID as your copy. If you haven't deleted the default Admin user from the Admins group (and added your logon name and PIN as a member of Admins), the person with the unauthorized copy has the same permissions as the default Admin user and can add or delete accounts in SYSTEM.MDA and permissions in the associated databases.

Prevent Admins from having irrevocable permissions

Access doesn't allow you to revoke the permissions of members of the Admins group for objects in databases that were created while a particular copy of SYSTEM.MDA was attached to Access. Even if you revoke permissions for individual objects in the database in the Permissions dialog, the revocation isn't effective for databases created while that SYSTEM.MDA was in use.

Create a new subdirectory to store the databases under development and to hold a new copy of the SYSTEM.MDA file that will be used with these databases. A separate copy of SYSTEM.MDA precludes members of the Admins group of one workgroup that use the group's SYSTEM.MDA file from possessing irrevocable permissions for databases in other workgroups that you are developing simultaneously.

Another way to prevent Admins from having irrevocable permissions for databases in another workgroup is to use the clean copy of SYSTEM.MDA described earlier or start with a new SYSTEM.MDA file copied from your Access distribution disks.

Use network security features to restrict users from opening files

If a user can launch a retail version of Access, the user can open any Access database that's accessible to him or her on the network, open the Database window, and add new objects to the database. Access 1.0 has no provisions to preclude users with no permissions for the database whatsoever from opening it with retail Access and viewing the names of the objects it contains or adding objects to the database. You must use network security features to restrict users from opening the database file.

The run-time version of Access, included in the Access Distribution Kit (ADK, which was in the beta test cycle when this book was written), doesn't display the Database window and doesn't allow users to create new database objects. Provide users who don't develop applications with copies of run-time Access and prevent them from being able to open the retail version of Access, if possible. Make sure, however, that you establish permissions for all users, because determined "snoopers" may acquire a retail copy of Access and try to bypass system security.

Revoke group permissions rather than individual permissions

All new users you add are members of the Users group. By default, the Users group provides to its members *implicit* full permissions for all objects in databases that the users can open. You need to revoke from the Users group permissions that don't apply to all users, such as Modify Data and Modify Definitions, so that you don't have to remove these permissions individually as you add new accounts to the Users group.

Also revoke the implicit Modify Data and Modify Definitions permissions of the Users group for each object in the database. This process can be tedious, however, if the database contains many objects. Revoking group permissions and then adding explicit permissions for individual users that need them takes substantially less time than revoking permissions on a user-by-user basis.

Grant *explicit* permissions to individual members of the Users group who need to modify data for data-entry operations. As a rule, don't grant Modify Definitions permission to members of the Users group. Modify Definitions permission is reserved to members of the Admins group and the object's owner.

Transfer ownership of objects with a new database

 The Access *User's Guide* doesn't discuss the concept of database object ownership as it applies to database security. The person who creates a database has irrevocable full permissions for all objects in the database. The person who adds a new object to a database, even if that object is only a combo box, has full, irrevocable permissions for that object. Members of the Admins group cannot revoke the permissions of the object's owner. The database owner cannot revoke the permissions of an object created by another user.

Irrevocable ownership permissions make operable the WITH OWNERACCESS OPTION statement, which by default is appended to Access SQL statements. WITH OWNERACCESS OPTION enables a user to run queries based on tables for which the user doesn't have *any* permissions.

The only way you can change the ownership of a database and the objects it contains is to open a new database while you or the person to whom you want to transfer ownership are logged on as a member of the Admins group.

Follow these steps:

1. Copy all objects from the existing database to the new database.

2. Verify that the new database is operational.

3. Make a backup copy of the old database.

4. Delete the old database.

Use this method when you transfer a database you have developed to the workgroup that will use the application. Attach the workgroup's SYSTEM.MDA file to your copy of Access and then create a new database in the workgroup directory. Import all the objects from the development database into the new database. You become the owner of the new database and the objects it contains. Members of the workgroup's Admins group then have full permissions for the database. The workgroup's database administrator then can assign permissions to users as required.

12

Taking Advantage of Libraries and Wizards

Libraries and wizards add features to Access that improve your productivity or extend Access's capabilities. To attach ;to your copy of Access, add *LibraryFile*.mda= to the [Libraries] section of your MSACCESS.INI file. After you attach a library to your copy of Access, its functions are available to any database you open.

Wizards are a special category of Access library, designed specifically for aiding in the design phase of your application. Wizards usually include a series of forms that prompt you for the information required for each step of a multi-step process. Most wizards add control objects to your forms or reports, but other wizards help you use some of Access's more arcane features, such as domain aggregate functions.

This chapter's tips are designed to help you obtain and use third-party libraries, wizards, and software development kits designed specifically for Access. Although software development kits (SDKs) and computer-aided software engineering (CASE) tools for Access technically aren't libraries or wizards, such tools are discussed in this chapter because they speed the process of designing effective Access applications.

Launch wizards and choose library functions easily from the Help menu

Each library or wizard has at least one entry point. An *entry point* is a function in one of the library's or wizard's modules that initiates the desired action. The entry point for the Database Analyzer library, supplied with Access, is the StartAnalyzer() function.

The documentation for Database Analyzer contained in the PSSKB.TXT file that accompanies Access suggests that you add a macro with a single action, **RunCode StartAnalyzer( )**, to launch the Database Analyzer. A better approach is to add a menu choice to the **Help** menu that calls the StartAnalyzer() function. When you add menu choices, you can use the functions in the library with any database you open, and you don't need to add a command button to a form or report to execute the function. Follow these steps to add a **Help** menu option:

1. Open your MSACCESS.INI file in Windows Notepad.

2. If you haven't done so already, add the line **analyzer.mda=** in the [Libraries] section. (The location of the line with respect to other library entries isn't important.) The .mda extension identifies attached database files, although you can use any extension you choose for libraries you write.

3. Add a new section to MSACCESS.INI, [**Menu Add-Ins**], after the last entry in the [Libraries] section. The surrounding square brackets are required to define a section entry in initialization (.INI) files.

4. Add the line **Anal&yzer==StartAnalyzer( )** under the [Menu Add-Ins] section.

The ampersand (&) underlines the *y* and assigns Alt+Y as the shortcut key for the Database Analyzer. The double equal sign (==) is required to execute a function.

5. Close Access, if it's running. Changes to MSACCESS.INI don't take effect until Access reads its newly modified initialization file on opening.

6. Launch Access, open a database, and then choose the Analyzer entry you just added from the Help menu. Database Analyzer's window appears.

You can use the preceding method to launch many third-party libraries. When you add the menu choice for the library's entry point to the Help menu, you don't need to add a RunCode macro to each database with which you want to use the library.

Note: You can start most—but not all—libraries and wizards from the Help menu. In some cases (such as the Menu Builder function of the FirstLib library described in a tip that follows), the function used as the entry point of the library requires argument values derived from objects in your currently open database. You cannot pass such values to a function with an entry in the [Menu Add-Ins] section of MSACCESS.INI.

Use Database Analyzer to document applications

The Database Analyzer library supplied with Access 1.0 is a rudimentary documentation application that extracts information from the MSSysObjects table of your database and creates a new table, @*ObjectClass*Details, for each database object class in your application.

Using Database Analyzer with macros is the subject of the tip "Document macros with Database Analyzer" in Chapter 6. In addition to macros, you can create detail tables that describe your database's tables, queries, forms, reports, and modules. You are left to your own devices, however, to design forms and reports that display and print the information in a useful format.

At the time this book was written, Kwery Corp. of Bellevue, Washington, was developing a product called Documenter that builds on the foundation of Database Analyzer to create professional-level forms and reports that fully describe your database objects. Expect other firms to release toolkits designed to accomplish similar objectives as the number of installed copies of Access increases.

Install libraries as read-only only when necessary

When you attach a library with a line in the [Libraries] section of MSACCESS.INI that includes the equal sign (=) without following characters, the library is installed with read-write capability. As a result, your application can modify data stored in tables of the library.

You need to run some libraries, such as WIZARD.MDA, as read-only libraries. Otherwise, the library may not load or produce the desired result. To designate a library as read-only, add **ro** after the equal sign (for example, wizard.mda=ro).

Note: If you have installed Access on a file server in a subdirectory with read-only permissions, you can install libraries with the ro attribute in the same read-only subdirectory. Libraries that require read-write capability

must be installed in a subdirectory with read-write permissions for all users who need to attach the library. You
also can make the Access subdirectory read-write and
then set the read-only attribute of all files except those for
read-write libraries. SYSTEM.MDA files must be located in
subdirectories with read-write permissions.

Reduce Access's memory consumption by disabling libraries you don't need

If your computer has less than 8M of RAM, running Access
together with mega apps such as Excel or Word for Windows can degrade performance. Each library or wizard
you attach increases Access's memory requirement.

Note: Excel and Word for Windows are called *mega apps*
because their .EXE files exceed 1M in size.

When you no longer need to use an attached library, de-
tach it from Access by preceding the `LibraryFile.mda=`
entry in the `[Libraries]` section of your MSACCESS.INI
file with a semicolon to disable the Database Analyzer:

    ;analyzer.mda=

After changing MSACCESS.INI, close and relaunch Access.
When you need the library again, delete the semicolon
and restart Access.

Improve Access performance for users lacking Modify Definitions permissions

Improve the performance of Access for users of your applications that don't have Modify Definitions permissions
by removing the `wizard.mda=ro` line from the `[Libraries]`
section of their MSACCESS.INI files. Access wizards are
used only in Design mode, not in Run mode.

Create a readable Zoom box by modifying **UTILITY.MDA**

You can replace the 8-point MS Sans Serif font used in the Zoom box with a more readable font, such as the 10-point System font used in the SQL window. To modify the Zoom box font, follow these steps:

1. Use File Manager to create a copy of UTILITY.MDA named MODUTILS.MDA.

    Note: Don't modify the original UTILITY.MDA. Always create a copy of UTILITY.MDA with a new name, and then modify the copy. That way, if you make changes that cause problems when you attach the new utility database, you can revert to the original and fix the problem in the modified file. You cannot open database objects in an attached library, so you need the new copy to modify.

2. Open MODUTILS.MDA in Access. Disregard the messages that say you are trying to open duplicate procedures. (You aren't allowed to have duplicate procedure or function names in a single Access database; function names in MODUTILS.MDA duplicate those in the attached UTILITY.MDA.)

3. Click the Forms button of the Database window, and then open ZoomForm in Design mode.

4. Click the unbound text box, and then change the typeface to System and the FontSize to 10 with the toolbar's combo boxes.

5. Close and save ZoomForm.

6. Close Access.

7. Open MSACCESS.INI in Windows Notepad. Change the c:\access\utility.mda line in the [Options] section to **c:\access\modutils.mda**.

8. Launch Access and test your modified Zoom form by opening a form that contains a property with a complex expression as its value.

Write domain aggregate expressions the easy way with the Domain Wizard

The domain aggregate functions, such as DSum( ), that enable you to find values in or calculate values from table fields or query columns have a syntax that isn't very intuitive. Dan Madoni of Microsoft Corp.'s Access Product Support Services created the Domain Wizard to create domain aggregate functions for you.

Download DOMAIN.ZIP from Library 15 (Third Party) of CompuServe's MSACCESS Forum. DOMAIN.ZIP includes DOMAIN.MDA and a text file, DOMAIN.TXT, that explains how to use the wizard to copy the text of the domain aggregate function you create to the Clipboard and then paste the function into a text box or other Access control object. The last step in creating a DLookup( ) function with the Domain Wizard is shown in figure 12.1.

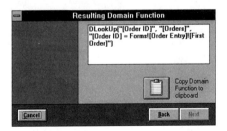

Fig. 12.1 *A DLookup( ) function created with the Domain Wizard.*

Create menus automatically with the MenuWizard

Creating special menus for your applications with a macro attached to the OnMenu event of your forms requires a series of AddMenu macros to add each menu bar and drop-down menu choice you want. Another library by Dan Madoni, MENU.MDA, automatically creates the macros that provide custom menus for your applications.

MENU.MDA and MENU.TXT (a short explanation of how to attach MENU.MDA) are included in the file MENU.ZIP, which you can download from Library 15 of CompuServe's MSACCESS Forum. The MenuWizard's window with entries that create a custom menu structure for an accounting application appears in figure 12.2. Click the Instructions button on the main form to display a form that explains how to use the MenuWizard.

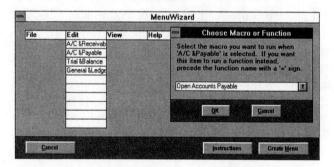

Fig. 12.2 *Creating a custom menu for an accounting application with the MenuWizard.*

Tap into productivity add-ins by downloading the FirstLib library

Download Andrew R. Miller's FirstLib library (FIRST.ZIP in Library 15 of CompuServe's MSACCESS Forum) to obtain FIRSTLIB.MDA and its accompanying instructions in

FIRSTLIB.TXT. The FirstLib library is an ingenious Access design toolkit that includes four basic functions:

- *Form Design Tool Palette* is a floating toolbar that creates sunken frames and shadow frames, resizes objects, makes selected controls the same size, aligns selected controls vertically and horizontally, and provides shortcut buttons for alignment options and the Bring to Front/Send to Back menu choices.

- *Menu Builder* presents a form, modeled on the Menu Design window of Visual Basic, to generate AddMenu macros. Menu Builder accomplishes the same end as the MenuWizard (described earlier in this chapter) in a manner to which Visual Basic programmers have become accustomed.

- *Macro-to-Module Converter* creates Access Basic code from your macros in the form of a text file that you can import into a module. Figure 12.3 shows the Converter's main (and only) form in the process of converting the Review Employee Orders macro of NWIND.MDB to a text file, EMP_ORDS.TXT. The Access Basic code in EMP_ORDS.TXT is shown in figure 12.4. The Macro-to-Module Converter is especially useful when you convert a database application to an Access library, because you cannot run a macro in a library.

- *Extended New Procedure Dialog* adds quite a few capabilities to the standard New Procedure option of Access's Edit menu. In this dialog, you can specify the name and type of the new procedure, as well as the data type of the return value, if you create a function. Each new procedure you create with this tool includes a standard header (similar to the first three lines shown in fig. 12.4). You can include standard error-trapping code as an option.

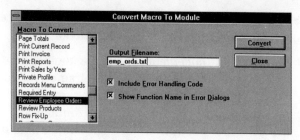

Fig. 12.3 *Converting the Review Employee Orders macro to a text file containing its equivalent in Access Basic code.*

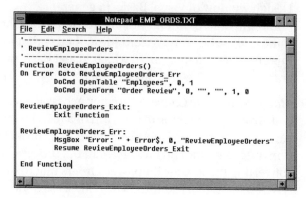

Fig. 12.4 *The Access Basic code created by converting the Review Employee Orders macro.*

Import the AutoKeys macro so that you can use shortcut keys in FirstLib

To use the shortcut keys to launch the tools in FirstLib, you need to import the AutoKeys macro from FIRSTLIB.MDA into your database, and then run the imported AutoKeys macro once. (You cannot execute macros in Access libraries, but you can include macros in a library for importing to applications that use the library.)

Alternatively, add the lines

> **FD &Tools==flib_OpenFDTools( ),**
> **&Macro to Module==flib_ConvertMacros( ),**
> **&New Procedure==flib_NewProc( )**

to the `[Menu Add-Ins]` section of MSACCESS.INI so that the FirstLib functions appear as **Help** menu choices. You cannot launch the Menu Builder function, `BuilderFormOnMenu`, from a Help menu choice because this function requires arguments, the values of which are derived from the form that is open when the function is called. (You don't need to import the AutoKeys macro to use the Menu Builder tool.)

Speed Access development by using custom toolbars

Access's toolbars that provide menu shortcuts are really Access forms in disguise; each toolbar is a form included in UTILITY.MDA. Thus, you can create a copy of UTILITY.MDA and then modify the toolbars to suit your own purposes.

Helen Feddema, an Access developer and author, took this approach to add several new functions to the toolbars she modified in NEWUTIL.MDA, which is included in UTILIT.ZIP, available in Library 15 of MSACCESS. Some of her additions include a handy Compile All button for modules, a substantial improvement to the Print Preview menu bar, and buttons to save changes to the design of your database objects. You can use the examples in NEWUTIL.MDA as the basis for creating your own set of custom toolbars to assist users of your applications.

Note: Feddema's custom toolbars had reached Version 4.0 when this book was written, but a later version likely will be available when you read this chapter. Check Library 15 of CompuServe's MSACCESS Forum for the latest version of UTILIT.ZIP before you download the file.

Add new functions to Access with special-purpose DLLs

Libraries for Access applications come in two types: Access database libraries and Windows dynamic link libraries, or DLLs. (Tips in Chapter 10, "Writing Access Basic Code that Works," describe how to use third-party DLLs with Access Basic.) Two DLLs designed specifically for use with Access and available for downloading from CompuServe's MSACCESS Forum are as follows:

- The Microsoft Access Data Definition Language library, MSADDL10.DLL, enables you to create new tables with Access Basic code, set primary key fields, and even establish default relationships between tables. MSADDL10.DLL is used by CASE tools, such as ServerWare's Access Designer, that aid in creating relational table structures for your Access applications. MSADDL.ZIP includes this library and documentation for the functions it contains.

- The SQL Pass-Through library, SPT.DLL, enables you to send non-Access-standard SQL statements to client-server RDBMS. You can activate stored procedures and send Transact-SQL statements to Microsoft and Sybase SQL Server with SPT.DLL. SPT.ZIP includes SPT.DLL and DEMO.MDB, a database to demonstrate the capabilities of SPT.DLL.

Declare prototypes of the functions in the Declarations section of your module, and use the correct syntax when you call the function. Declaring and calling functions in DLLs is discussed in Chapter 10, "Writing Access Basic Code that Works." Some Access libraries, such as OUTPUTAS.MDA (the subject of tips in Chapter 8, "Printing Professional Reports"), also require an accompanying Windows DLL. In this case, the function prototypes are declared in the modules of the Access library.

Check the MSACCESS forum regularly for libraries and wizards

When this book was written, new libraries and wizards were appearing in CompuServe's MSACCESS Forum at the rate of at least one a week. To display a current list of wizards authored by the Microsoft PSS staff and independent developers, BROWSE ALL libraries using the keyword WIZARD. You can download a database application that contains a catalog of all the files available in the forum (CATLOG.ZIP in Library 1, Index and Info) to locate all the libraries and wizards available.

Use commercial Access products as models of professional design

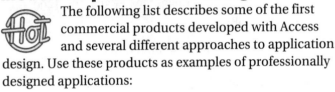 The following list describes some of the first commercial products developed with Access and several different approaches to application design. Use these products as examples of professionally designed applications:

- Access to Word is a commercial Access wizard published by Kwery Corp. (P.O. Box 6726, Bellevue, WA 98008-0726, 206-644-7830, fax 206-644-8409) that aids in using Access tables as the data source for Word for Windows print-merge operations. Access to Word includes Word for Windows macros, a wizard file, and a custom DLL, and makes extensive use of DDE to perform its print-merge duties.

- WorkGroup Solutions' Time and Billing/EIS is a complete Access database system that you can use "as is" to maintain records of time spent by you and others on specific products. You can create invoices for clients or use the reports to maintain records of the development cost of your Access applications.

Contact WorkGroup Solutions at 2366 Eastlake Ave., Suite 325, Seattle, WA 98102, telephone 206-726-9377, fax 206-726-9278.

■ MTX International's Accounting SDK for Access is a complete, integrated accounting application with General Ledger, Accounts Receivable, Accounts Payable, and Payroll modules. You can modify the form designs, macros, and Access Basic source code to suit your particular requirements. You can add or attach, for example, a custom order entry or inventory control system to the existing application that interacts with the Accounts Receivable module. For more information, contact MTX International, Inc. at 98 Inverness Drive, East, Suite 110, Englewood, CO 80112, telephone 800-888-6894 or 303-790-1400, fax 303-790-4058.

■ Skil-Trak is a database application that maintains descriptions and prices for courses offered by training vendors and in-house training staffs, the skills taught by these courses, prerequisites, and course schedules. An employee skills checklist and tables of skills required for specific job classifications are included. When you plan to assign an employee to a new job classification, for example, Skil-Trak checks to see what courses are available to upgrade the employee's skills for the new classification. For more information, contact Meliora Systems, Inc. at 95 Allens Creek Road, Suite 302, Rochester, NY 14618, telephone 716-461-1900, fax 716-461-1989.

■ Access Designer is a computer-aided software engineering (CASE) tool designed to create Access tables for your applications. Access Designer is supplied as an .EXE file, not as an Access database. Access Designer includes a repository to store facts, objects, and rules that determine the database design. The content of the repository is expressed in common English terms rather than in the form of entity-relationship diagrams (ERDs) or other complex graphical database schema representations. For more information, contact ServerWare, Inc. at 11911 NE 1st St., Suite 306, Bellevue, WA 98005, telephone 206-454-7535, fax 206-454-7696.

Index

functions
    DLLs, 198
    Format( ), 109
    library, Help menu, 20
    Mid( ), 55-56
    MsgBox( ), 86
    RECNO( ) (xBASE),
        emulating, 45
    SQL aggregrate, 64
    StartAnalyzer( ), 188-189
    sub-procedures, 158-159
    user-defined, 156
    utility, 157
    Windows API, 169-170
    WritePrivateProfileString( ),
        170-171

G

GoToControl actions, imitating labels, 79-80
graphic objects
    linking, 34
    tables, 33
graphs
    creating, 131-132, 137-139
    hiding title, 146-147
    linked, 145-146
    linking to forms, 143-144
    logarithmic Y-axis scaling,
        133-134
    Run mode, 139-140
    single-line, 132
    y-axis values, 140
GraphWizard, 131, 136-137
    Version 1.0, linking graphs
        to forms, 143-144
grids, spacing, Design mode,
    92

H

headings, fixed column, 66
Help menu
    library functions, 20
    starting wizards and
        libraries, 188-189
Hewlett-Packard laser
    printers, 118
hiding
    forms, 95
    text boxes, 101
hierarchical forms, 93-94
HP LaserJet II family of
    printers, 120
Hungarian notation, 153

I

Immediate Window, 150-151
imported tables, developing
    applications, 44
importing
    data
        Clipboard, 49-50
        Excel, 48
    files
        comma- and tab-
            separated text, 48-49
        FoxPro 2.x DBF, 52
    tables, 43-44
        Btrieve, 46, 53
        exclusive file access,
            43-44
        Paradox, 46
    text files, 49
    worksheets, 47
index files, applications,
    Clipper, 51-52

summary, queries, 65
updating, 68
tabular data, importing,
49-50
template databases, 116
templates, reports, 115-116
text boxes
expressions containing
field names, 105
hiding, 101
passing criteria to queries,
105-106
read-only, 100
subform, macros, 113
unbound, 79-80, 102-104
text editors, 49
Text fields, 30
text files, importing, 48-49
thumbnails, 36
Time and Billing/EIS database system, 199
toolbars, speeding Access
development, 197
tools, CASE, 187
Access Designer, 200
Totals command
(View menu), 64, 69
trackballs, 15-16
transaction processing,
165-166
TrueType fonts, 118-120
typefaces, 119-120

U

unbound text boxes, 79-80,
102-104
updating tables, 68

user names, command line,
21-22
user-defined functions, 156
Users command
(Security menu), 181
UTILITY.MDA file, 180
Zoom boxes, 192-193

V

validation
field-by-field, 85-89
macros, 40-41, 84-85
rules, 41
problems, 70
Validation Rule property,
40-41
Validation Text property, 41
values
deleting duplicate, 69-70
freezing, importing
worksheets, 47
key field, dBASE files, 45
Variant data type, 152
VCR buttons, *see* record
selectors
virtual memory, 13
Visual Basic, WIN30API.TXT,
167-168
Visual Basic code, 171-172

W

WHERE clause, SQL, 61
Windows, swap files, 13
windows
MDI (multiple document
interface) child, 96-97
modal, 96-97
modeless, 96-97
pop-up, 96-97